"The Most Important Promise I Ever Made."

"It was a promise to God and I made it while holding the hand of step-daughter Cheryl, who was lying near death in a hospital in Tucson. She'd been in a terrible automobile accident and her body was shattered. She was in a deep coma, and the doctors have her no chance at all. But I wouldn't, I couldn't give up.

"So I stayed with her in intensive care. Day after day, holding her hand, talking to her, telling her that I loved her, that we all loved her. The nurses said it was useless, that she couldn't hear me. But I didn't listen.

"When Cheryl finally woke up, she told me things I'd said to her. And I spoke to God. I promised God that if he would let her live, I would do something useful with my life, something to make the world a little better because I'd been there.

"Cheryl lived and I've tried to keep that promise every since."

MICHAEL LANDON
HIS TRIUMPH AND TRAGEDY

AILEEN JOYCE

ZEBRA BOOKS
KENSINGTON PUBLISHING CORP.

To Shaddie, my funny, feisty and faithful companion of 14 years.

ZEBRA BOOKS

are published by

Kensington Publishing Corp.
475 Park Avenue South
New York, NY 10016

First printing: August, 1991

Printed in the United States of America

Introduction

It's been thirty-two years since Michael Landon first rode across the television screen as "Little Joe" in "Bonanza," blazing a trail that would ultimately lead him to the forefront of American television.

Michael Landon was unique. He was the only person in the annals of television history to ever successfully wear four hats — writer, producer, director, and actor — and to inspire millions of Americans to try and live better lives through his TV movies and series. In doing so, he became an American icon, a living symbol of understanding, openness, kindness, and warmth. And, indeed, he had those qualities.

He was a complicated man, whose tremendous ego and overwhelming need to control the world around him reflected the best and the worst of human nature. He was, as a magazine writer so aptly described, a man who had "tried and failed to swim against the dark tides of his own nature" in what had been a futile venture from the beginning.

In the pages ahead we'll explore the various personas, public and private, of this one-of-a-kind TV *wunderkind,* beginning with his unhappy childhood through his death from cancer of the pancreas on July 1, 1991. What you will discover is that like most people, Michael Landon was the sum total of his experiences — experiences which gave him strength and courage throughout his life up to his last moments.

A perfectionist in an imperfect world, Michael fervently believed in his vision of the inherent goodness of mankind, a vision he shared weekly from the beginning of "Little House" in 1974 through the end of "Highway to Heaven" fifteen years later. The roles he played represented what Michael Landon wanted to be, not necessarily what he was. Nevertheless, he became a role model for millions of parents and their children, with whom he enjoyed a special relationship.

Whether consciously or subconsciously, Michael had cast himself as the savior he had so desperately yearned for in his childhood. In his mind, he was The White Knight on a white stallion, riding to the rescue of those who were unable to defend themselves. Sometimes the underdogs were adults; but most frequently they were children, helpless against injustice and cruelty . . . just as Michael had been helpless in his fight to survive an abusive childhood. It was a pattern which repeatedly manifested itself both on and off the set.

What emerges from this portrait is a classic Hollywood tale of a man filled with unresolved pain and anguish, driven to succeed, yet victimized by childhood experiences he could harness creatively but never overcome emotionally. The result was an unvanquished need to control everything and everyone in his world, including himself.

On the surface, Michael Landon had everything money and fame could buy; but beneath that surface there was a nagging emptiness that propelled him to repeatedly attempt to realize his dreams, his values, his vision of how the world *should* be through the powerful medium of television.

Along the way there were severe bouts of depression and angry outbursts, pill-taking and heavy drinking, and two divorces. Yet, through it all, Michael always emerged triumphant. Whatever his shortcomings, the unalterable fact is that very few people, other than perhaps Walt Disney, have ever devoted as much of their lives to creating wholesome family programming as Michael Landon.

As a child, he had faced the worst the world had to offer and he had survived despite the odds. As an adult he had risen to heights greater than he could ever have imagined, again against all odds. As a result, he had no fear of living — and no fear of dying.

A positive force forged out of adversity, Michael Landon was an inspirational blend of hope, strength, and courage. He will not be easily forgotten by those who shared his dream of a better, more kindly world.

One

Michael Landon was born Eugene Maurice Orowitz on October 31, 1936, in Forest Hills, New York, the youngest of two children from the unhappy union of Peggy O'Neill, a Broadway show girl, and Eli Maurice Orowitz, a Broadway publicist. Nicknamed "Ugey," East Coast slang for his real name, Eugene grew up in the blue-collar community of Collingswood, New Jersey, where the family had moved when he was only six years old.

Despite both of his parents having been involved in show business, Ugey was anything but "star material" throughout his school days. According to those who "knew-him-when," Eugene had all the attributes of a loser. He was short and rail thin for his age. So thin, in fact, that he often wore several pairs of pants to give the illusion of added weight. Sometimes he would even wear a sweatshirt beneath his regular shirt for added girth. Making matters even worse, he had ears that stuck out like an elephant's, which only served to accentuate his thin, pale face.

As often is the case, the child who needs love and affection the most is the one who gets it the least. This was certainly true for Eugene, whose parents ignored him but doted on his older sister, Evelyn, who was so pretty she entered every local and regional beauty pageant and ultimately became a Miss New Jersey.

From all outside appearances the Orowitz family of Collingswood, New Jersey, was a typically middle-class family of four. They lived in a comfortable two-story, red-brick colonial home at 632 Newell Lake Drive, a shady street of similar homes, all set on tree-covered lots of neatly trimmed shrubbery and nicely mowed yards. It was a safe neighborhood at a time in America when people didn't lock their doors, neighbors spoke to each other, and the streets and playgrounds still belonged to the children.

Eli Orowitz had held down several jobs in New York prior to marrying the former Peggy O'Neill. He'd been a writer, then a radio announcer, who went by the name of Mr. Emo, on the "Lady Esther" show in New York in the 1930s. For a while he had headed the East Coast publicity department of RKO Radio Pictures. At one point he also had been a personal publicist for several major stars, including Gene Autry. By the time the family moved to Collingswood, however, Eli was working as the district manager of a theater chain. It was a job he felt was beneath him, but with four mouths to feed, Eli didn't feel he could afford to be choosy.

Peggy Orowitz, who had been a Ziegfeld Follies chorus girl when she met and married Eli, stayed at home, where she spent her days tending to the house and to the children, little Eugene and his older sister, Evelyn. Although Michael would later characterize his mother as "a sad, gloomy person, always looking for the bad, never looking for the good," neighbors remember Peggy Orowitz happily belting out Broadway songs at full throttle as she washed dishes in the family kitchen.

To the neighbors, Mrs. Orowitz was a typical mother, making ice tea for all the kids with whom she also was known to infrequently jump rope and sometimes give impromptu tap dancing lessons. Beneath this veil of normality, however, there were problems. Big problems that none of the neighbors realized until years later, when they read about them in Michael's newspaper and magazine interviews. Even then, it was difficult for the people who had resided near the Orowitz family to believe what they read.

"They seemed pretty normal, average, ordinary people to me," recalled Alice Pelo, who lived only four houses away from the Orowitz family home. "I lived next to them for twelve years, from 1940 until they moved to California in 1952. So, although Gene was three years younger than me, I knew him and his family quite well. When we were growing up we liked to listen to the radio and those great old serials in the afternoon, like "Tom Mix," "The Green Hornet." We didn't have television until 1947 or so. Neither did Eugene's family. But Eugene's father was managing some movie theaters, so every time there was a new movie, the whole family would go see it. Once in a while they took me, too. And I remember going once to see Eugene and his sister, Evelyn, in a play staged by their drama teacher. As I recall, both of them were studying drama; but that's the only thing I ever remember seeing Eugene in, which I guess is why I was so surprised when he went to Hollywood and became such a big star. I don't think anyone in Collingswood would have ever imagined that happening."

"I lived next door to the Orowitz family, but I was ten years older than Eugene so we weren't playmates," recalled George Roney. "He was a delightful youngster and I always thought he'd be a comedian because he seemed to be so quick and had a great sense of humor. That was his forte. Of course, he was always in the shadow of his older sister, Evelyn, who always seemed to be in a beauty contest, which she always seemed to win. I think it was because of Evelyn, in fact, that the family moved to California. I believe they made the move to further Evelyn's career, but I could be wrong."

Although Eli was a nonpracticing Jew who claimed to have been in a synagogue only once in his life (for Eugene's bar mitzvah), Peggy grew to hate his religion after the marriage. After a while, Eli began to dislike Catholics, especially his staunchly Catholic wife. As a result the two fought bitterly and unrelentingly about religion in front of Michael and his older sister. "Then the rabbi and the priest would get together . . . and *they* would argue," Michael laughingly recalled. "It was a big mess."

Most of the time, however, Eli and Peggy simply wouldn't speak to each other, except through Eugene.

"They'd go six weeks at a time without so much as a hello," Michael would later recall, adding, "There was no arguing, no nothing. We never hugged or showed any emotion. My mother would say, 'Tell your father that dinner is ready.' And my father would be standing four feet away!"

As Michael once told a friend, "A Jew who hates a Catholic should never marry a Catholic who hates a Jew. Looking back, though, I see that it really wasn't a problem of religion. It was a problem of not having anything in common. Besides, they didn't really love each other. I don't ever remember them sleeping together. I mean, I have an older sister, so I know they had sex. But I never saw them sleep together. The priest had told my mother she couldn't have Holy Communion if she slept with my father. So she didn't and, truthfully, I don't think my father was particularly disappointed."

The major problem in the Orowitz family, however, was the mental health of Peggy Orowitz, which, even in the best of times, was not very stable. In her mind, Peggy O'Neill had given up a flourishing show business career, possibly because she was pregnant with Evelyn, to marry a man with whom she had nothing in common and whomshe eventually came to hate. She saw Eli as a weakling, a loser who'd had a number of jobs but was never quite successful at any of them. Frustrated and angry at having settled for so much less than she felt she deserved, she focused her increasing bitterness on Eli and then on their curly-dark-haired son.

Evelyn, on the other hand, resembled Peggy's side of the family. She was fair-haired, fair-skinned, and looked Irish, all of which made her special in the eyes of her unhappy mother. As a result, Peggy O'Neill was determined that Evelyn would have the opportunities she, Peggy, had sacrificed for an ill-begotten marriage. Thus she doted on Evelyn, giving her all of her attention, while dismissing Eugene as the son of a father who was the reason for her unhappiness. And when she could no longer torture Eli, who had grown immune to her venomous attacks, she turned her attention to Eugene, making his life something akin to a tale straight out of Charles Dickens.

"The day I was bar mitzvahed was a great day. I had finished the bar mitzvah and we were having a small cake and a little party at home when, suddenly, my mother called me into another room. Now you have to understand," Michael once told a writer, "that I was thirteen years old and had just gone through the whole bar mitzvah thing, learning the chanting, the Hebrew, the whole megillah, riding my bicycle to Haddon Heights every day for this big event.

"When I went into the room, she said, 'I thought you'd like to know, son, that you are not Jewish. I haven't told you or anyone else, but when you were a baby, I took you out and had you baptized Catholic! This whole day has been a joke!' "

As an adult, Michael chose to find the humor in his mother's neurotic shenanigans. "My mother had a lot of mental problems but she was amazing," he once confided, with a sad smile, "and as I look back, I've got to laugh at some of the things she did. She'd take an ambulance to buy a loaf of bread, and it would cost one hundred and seventy-five dollars. And she was always saying she was going to kill herself. It was like, if it's Tuesday it must be suicide day."

But, in truth, as a helpless child totally at the mercy of his mother, Michael's childhood was a vivid nightmare come to life. He was a master of understatement when, in an early 1970s interview in the now-defunct *Coronet* magazine, he told the writer: "My home was filled with conflict that I absolutely could not understand as a child."

It would have been difficult for anyone, adult or child, to understand the manic machinations of Mrs. Orowitz, who was constantly threatening to kill either herself, or Eugene. Her favorite form of suicide involved the kitchen stove. Returning from school, Eugene would find her down on her knees, her head in the oven and the gas on.

"She'd stick her head in the oven, but she always had knee pads on the floor so she wouldn't hurt her knees," Michael once laughingly recalled, adding, "or she'd have a window open."

Perhaps the most memorable of his mother's frequent suicide attempts occurred when Eugene was only ten years old. The family was taking a rare vacation in California and staying at a motel overlooking the ocean. As it turned out, it was the only vacation the foursome ever took together.

"My father had gotten up early and gone to a restaurant to get fresh orange juice for my mother and sister," Landon recalled in a recent interview. "But my sister refused to drink it, and she and my father had an argument. Then my mother went into one of her weird moods.

Her eyes opened wide and she seemed to just float across the floor and out the door in her nightgown. While I was pleading with my father and sister not to argue, I looked out the window and saw my mother walking toward the water. And I knew what she was going to do, or at least try to do."

Eugene raced outside. Running up to her, he begged her not to go into the water, to come back inside with him and have breakfast instead. His pleas fell on deaf ears. Peggy Orowitz kept determinedly walking across the beach and into the raging surf, totally oblivious to the frantic sobs of the young boy tugging at her arm.

As the water grew deeper and deeper, Eugene began to panic because he didn't know how to swim and the water was almost up to his neck. Desperate to save himself and his mother, he swung his fist as hard as he could, hitting her in the face. He continued punching her until she finally fell over in the waves. At that point he managed to drag her back onto the beach.

"I pulled her onto the beach and sat on top of her while she was crying for my sister. I swear to God, forty-five minutes later my mother and sister were in their bathing suits, playing in the sand as though nothing had happened. My father did nothing, except to look pathetic. And I'm on the beach, at the water's edge, vomiting." Later that day Eugene made a solemn promise to himself:

He vowed that *his* life was going to be far, far different from that of his parents.

Adding to Eugene's childhood misery was the fact that his family was one of only a handful of Jewish families living in Collingswood, a working-class community. As a result, he was often taunted by the other kids who called him a "Jew bastard."

"I was one of two Jewish kids in my class," he once recalled, "and when all the other kids were released to attend religious instructions on Wednesdays, I'd stay behind. I'd be given the job of cleaning the blackboards and the erasers, which made me feel like a leper with a bell around my neck.

"But it wasn't just at school that I felt this way. Guys used to drive by me in their cars and shout, 'Jew bastard! Jew bastard!' Maybe they were yelling, 'You bastard!' But it sure sounded like 'Jew bastard' to me. Kids used to feel the front of my head to see if I had horns. I mean, I'm not kidding, they really believed that Jew had horns under their hair. And then, when I was in high school, I remember going to pick up a date and having her father come to the door and announce, 'My daughter's not going out with a Jews,' before slamming the door in my face. So, yeah, you could say being a Jew in Collingswood wasn't very thrilling."

Forced to live with an abusive anti-Semitic mother, tormented by strangers outside the home, and an outcast at school, it's hardly surprising that Eugene became a chronic bed wetter. Fearful that the few friends he *did* have would discover his humiliating secret, Eugene would never spend the night at friends' homes, a situation which further isolated the lonely little boy.

In a misguided attempt to stop his bed-wetting, Mrs. Orowitz began hanging the soiled sheets from Eugene's bedroom window so that his classmates, passing by on their way home from school, could witness his shameful secret. "I'd race home to drag them in before the other kids could see them," Landon recalled. However, his efforts to hide his secret were futile. When hanging the stained sheets from the front bedroom window failed to halt the problem, Peggy Orowitz tied the discolored sheet to his back and forced him to walk to school that way. It wasn't until Ugey was fourteen years old that "the problem" disappeared.

Years later Ugey would write, direct, and star in an NBC television movie based on his recollections of the embarrassment and shame he felt about his uncontrollable bed-wetting and the subsequent humiliation he suffered by the actions of his mother. Titled *The Loneliest Runner,* the film was televised in 1976. By that time, of course, he had become Michael Landon, one of the most powerful forces in television, and Collingswood was mostly a distant memory. Nevertheless, the scars were profound.

"My mother," Landon would confess years

later, "was a stabber, a kicker, and a wacko. She was totally off her rocker as far back as I can remember. She was very abusive. One time she came after me with a knife while I was in my jockey shorts. It was frightening because you never knew what you were going to be greeted with when you came home from school. She'd sit on the sofa in her nightgown—she always wore her nightgown when she was upset, when she was getting ready to try and kill herself—holding a Bible, asking God to kill me.

"One time," he continued, "when I was about fifteen years old, I was standing in front of the Triangle drugstore, talking with some guys and a couple of girls when, all of a sudden, a cab pulled up and out came my mother, standing in the freezing cold with just her nightgown on. She had a hanger in her hand and started whacking the hell out of me. She was calling the girls tramps while she was hitting me. I looked around and said to the astonished girls, 'Well, I gotta take my mother home now.' And we went home."

Peggy Orowitz was a neurotic woman who probably should have been under a doctor's care and medicated for her bouts of madness. However, in the forties and early fifties, when Eugene was growing up, this kind of behavior was swept under the carpet, if at all possible. There was no cure, other than hospitalization, for manic depressives such as Peggy Orowitz. According to Landon, his mother did seek help in her later years, but "not one psychiatrist did a damn thing to help her. And no one was ever able to diagnose her problem." As a result, she went unchecked, untreated, and unhappily down her path of self-destruction, leaving a totally dysfunctional family in her wake.

Peggy Orowitz didn't leave this earth until 1981, but her son had received his inheritance years before. It was a lifetime legacy of depression, anger, and frustration, and a desperate need to control the world in which he lived and worked. When that world was out of control, so was Eugene, and he would find himself trying to escape his inner pain through drinking and, at one point, prescription drugs. Peggy Orowitz was the source of his strength, independence, drive—and lifelong pain.

Her willing accomplice in this ongoing madness, of course, was Eli Orowitz, whose silence and abdication as head of the household only served to increase his wife's fury and to further isolate his shy, lonely, alienated son, Ugey.

Eli apparently was a strict parent, but he was rarely at home. Like his son, he chose to go elsewhere and spent most of his time at work, managing two movie theaters, The Savar and The Grand, in nearby Camden. Unlike his wife, Eli was not a physically abusive parent. "He never disciplined me really, and he only hit me once. He didn't want to hit me then," Landon once told an interviewer, "but my mother goaded him into it. He didn't even know how to hit me because, by the time this happened, I was six inches taller than he was. So he slapped me with the back of his hand and a ring he was wearing cut my lip. I started to bleed, and although it didn't bother me, my father started to cry and left the room. I was really glad it had happened because it was the first time in my life I'd ever seen my father show any emotion."

Although Eli Orowitz was not physically abusive, he nevertheless failed to offer any recognizable love, any kind of safe harbor to his son, or any emotional balance to the erratic conduct of his wife. He was a solemn, rather stoic man as isolated from the world around him as was his young son. According to the recollections of a former neighbor, Eli also had a strange rule that Eugene could not take any of his toys out of his bedroom. "One day, when we were about seven years old," recalled Joan Moss, a former playmate, "I was over at the Orowitzes' house when his father arrived home early. I knew his father didn't like other kids to be in the house, so I left. We had been playing with some of his toys in the living room and I could hear Ugey's father screaming at him about it from my house. It went on for quite a while."

Asked about his relationship with his father years later, Landon acknowledged that he had "had no relationship" with Eli Orowitz. "We didn't know each other," he explained. "He worked constantly as the district manager for several movie theaters. So by the time he got up

22

in the morning, I was already on my way to school. I saw my father for perhaps an hour a day at the dinner table."

If life was a miserable existence at home, it was equally dismal away from home. Shy, skinny, and introverted, Eugene was an outsider at school. In elementary school he was a well-dressed, quiet, and polite straight A student who was well-liked by his teachers. But he was not accepted by his peers, had few friends, and usually ate lunch alone in the school cafeteria.

"I wasn't popular with the rest of the kids, and that hurt me. I desperately wanted people to like me." Unhappy at home and dreading the hours he spent at school, Eugene retreated into a fantasy world of comic books, solitary walks, and the age-old fantasy of "Someday I'll be somebody and you'll all be sorry."

"As a kid," he would later tell a newspaper writer, "I'd spend my whole summer never seeing another kid. One of the great joys of my life was going fishing. I'd get up when it was still dark, take a little sandwich and an apple, and leave before anyone else was up. I had a little cave I had dug in a place I called the North Woods. It was down at the end of Newall Creek, not far from where I lived. Anyway, I'd put little canned goods in my cave, and I'd stay in there and daydream about how the Germans had taken over Collingswood and how I was there, hiding out in the woods; about how I'd be the Green Lantern, a guy with a bow and arrow, swinging on vines over the riverbank, shooting Nazis, and saving this particular girl I happened to like. It was all fantasy but . . . I wanted to stay and live in that cave the rest of my life."

When he grew older, Eugene divided his time between fishing from sunrise to sunset and panhandling in nearby Philadelphia, Pennsylvania. As he once explained, "I'd hitchhike to Philadelphia, where I'd sleep for the weekend in a farmhouse. I'd wear ripped clothes, dirty my face, and stand on the corner with the bums. I liked those guys because they treated me like an adult. And since I was a pathetic little twelve-year-old, I always got a full cup of coins. Then I'd take the guys for steak sandwiches. Weekends like those gave me strength and independence. Besides, anything was certainly better than being at home."

Bright, restless, and intellectually unchallenged, Eugene had always been something of a hardheaded daredevil. While in grade school, for example, he broke both of his ankles by jumping off a house while playing tag. "The falling was fun," he later laughed, "but not the landing." Another time, when he was about eleven years old, he was showing off, running back and forth under a swing while a playmate was on it, and he ran smack into the swing in midflight, a collision which sent him to the doctor for stitches. Not long after that, again showing off, he hit himself in the head with a wild swing from a golf club.

Starved for the attention and the affection he was missing at home, Eugene became the "classroom cutup," raising it almost into an art form when he entered high school. As the class clown, Eugene entertained classmates, to the horror of his teachers, by hanging out a second-story window by his fingertips. He also became famous for his English class book reports, all of which, according to Tom Rizzi, a high school pal, were "phoney. He would never read any of the books assigned to us. Instead he'd make up titles, authors, and phoney plots, and it always worked. He was always able to pull the wool over the teacher's eyes. It was amazing."

It was during that period of his life that Eugene also became famous for his crazy bets, such as the time he bet another boy that he could eat fifteen hamburgers. The boy bet him he couldn't and offered to pay for the hamburgers if Eugene wanted to try. Eugene accepted the offer and astounded everyone by calmly downing the burgers one by one in record time. Another claim to fame for the ingenious Eugene was his ability to outrace a car—on foot.

"He would say to these kids with cars: 'I'll bet you two dollars I can beat you to that telephone pole over there,' " recalled another classmate, adding, "and, by God, he'd do it. The pole was about thirty yards away, but he'd beat them every time."

But beneath the humor and adolescent high jinks, there lurked an anger that Ugey Orowitz would carry with him long after he had become Michael Landon, the handsome, rich, and famous television actor.

In fact, it was while he was in high school that the ugly side of the future Michael Landon first reared its nasty head. All the resentment the "polite, quiet" youngster had previously held in check began to surface. Where there had been depression, there was now rage. Eugene became rebellious and began deliberately starting fights. The boys were always his age and his size and he didn't always win the battle, but the fights allowed him to let off steam, to get rid of that knot in his stomach.

Once, according to a high school friend, Eugene went into a frenzy and unnecessarily beat another teenager to a bloody pulp, while several dozen of his classmates stood in a circle, watching the spectacle in amazement.

"The other kid wouldn't give up," recalled the friend, "and blood was going all over Ugey's jacket. It was just pathetic. It was one of the longest, bloodiest fights I ever saw in my life, with Ugey just punching this kid to death." Eugene proudly wore the blood-spattered jacket for several months after the fight. It was his trophy, his manhood, his red badge of courage. It was the beginning of a new life. Eugene Orowitz had begun his rites of passage and was on his way to taking over control of his own life.

His father might be the kind of man who allowed people to walk all over him, but his son was not of the same ilk. Eugene made another solemn vow to himself: He would never take abuse from anybody ever again.

"Yeah, I changed when I went to high school. When I first entered high school my self-esteem was in the gutter. I was a nothing person going no place. I was small and shy, and I had these strange tics. I made gulping noises and I did these weird motions with my arms. I don't know why. I guess it was just nervousness. I hadn't been popular in grade school because I got straight A's and the other kids were jealous because the teachers liked me. So I decided that since I didn't think I was going to college, it would be better if I weren't so smart. I didn't have any friends so I thought maybe I could get some by acting like a clown. So I became a real hell-raiser—ditching, fighting, getting kicked out, and getting a lot of F's," he recalled. "I was real bad in high school, so bad I got kept back a grade and had to do my sophomore year all over again. That was embarrassing. I was the object of ridicule, and it was one fistfight after another. I was treated like I was subhuman. I graduated ranked at 299th out of 301," he said, proudly adding, "but they elected me vice president of the class."

Despite his hell-raising, Ugey blossomed in high school. He developed strength and independence and the keen sense of humor he would carry with him throughout his life. It was a sense of humor for which he was noted on the sets of his TV series. It was a humor that masked his dark side, that could win him friends or drive away enemies. He could be playful, then turn cutting and sarcastic with the blink of an eye if he felt threatened or intimidated by anything or anyone in any way. Humor was Eugene's lifelong defense against a world that had too often proven itself to be cruel and uncaring.

Two

As he entered his junior year of high school, having been held back a year as a sophomore because of his poor grades, Eugene Orowitz, by his own admission, was "a nobody going nowhere." He now had friends, thanks to his deliberate stupidity in the realm of education; but nothing much else had changed. Life at home remained the same miserable nightmare. He was still being called a "Jew bastard" from time to time. And there were still parents who, when they discovered he was Jewish, refused to let their daughters go out with him.

Still a 126-pound weakling, he was as big a failure in gym class as he was in the classroom. He'd gone out for football, but didn't stick with it. He also tried out for baseball and track, but he didn't continue in those sports, either. He just wasn't a team player. It made him uncomfortable that everyone else seemed to be buddies, pals. They had a camaraderie that, somehow, he just didn't have.

Then something incredible happened that changed his life and his self-image completely and forever. It was near the end of the school year, in late spring, when Eugene's gym teacher Maurey Dickinson took the class out on the practice field and had everybody take a turn at throwing a javelin. Although he was convinced he would embarrass himself in front of the bigger, stronger guys, Ugey took his turn at throwing, and to the astonishment of the coach and his fellow classmates, he threw the javelin the length of the field and into the stands, at least thirty feet farther than anyone else. In only a moment, Eugene had found something that he could do better than other people. It was, he later explained, "something I could grab onto. And I grabbed."

Eugene begged the teacher to let him take the javelin home, during summer vacation, so that he could practice throwing. The teacher relented. Eugene carried the javelin home and began throwing it over and over, until his arm was sore. It was then that the puny teenager began working out, doing exercises to strengthen his upper torso. That summer, Eugene went to see Victor Mature in the title role of the biblical epic, *Sam-*

son and Delilah, at one of his father's movie houses.

Caught up in the legend of Samson, Eugene became convinced that if he let his hair grow he, too, would have super strength. He stopped getting haircuts and soon his shaggy brunette locks were shoulder length, so long that at one point, his hair fell all the way to the middle of his back. Long hair became Ugey's trademark. His hair, he believed throughout his adult life, was a source of strength, of power. As a result, he never had his hair cut short again. Besides, it hid his protruding ears.

Obsessed with his newfound talent, Eugene practiced throwing the javelin for hours every day. The endless practice ultimately paid off and he became a top thrower for the school, winning the admiration of his challengers and his teammates as he first became regional champion, then state champion.

"My ability to throw the javelin led me to believe that I could become somebody," he once confided to a friend. "I was literally transformed. It gave me total confidence and the urge to look for new worlds to conquer, and it brought me a lot of recognition and the offer of scholarships to colleges all over the country. But I still couldn't get any praise out of my dad. Then one day," he continued, "my dad read in the newspaper that I was the number one high school javelin thrower in the United States. But he didn't have the slightest idea what a javelin

31

was. So he showed up at the athletic field when we were having a meet.

"I'll never forget it. I came running down and I'm feeling like I'm really going to whip that javelin and I throw it fifty feet farther than anyone else in the competition. Well, my dad looks, then he turns and walks back to his car and drives away. It was like he was thinking, How could a person make a living doing that?' I was so disappointed because, well, I thought that he would be so proud of me, and he wasn't. Or if he was, he certainly never showed it."

Despite his father's lack of praise and approval, Eugene continued to focus all of his energies on the javelin. The effort paid off in his senior year, when Eugene threw the javelin farther than any other high schooler in America, and set a New Jersey state record that went unchallenged for the next decade. He felt invincible. The mouse had finally roared.

"You've heard of people who want to have their good side photographed?" he would later joke. "Well, I wanted to hide behind my left arm. I was a skinny, funny-looking kid, a 125-pound weakling with one enormous left arm from javelin throwing."

Unlike his first years of high school, which he admittedly wasted, Eugene's junior and senior years were spent working nights at a soup cannery, saving money, and dreaming about the Olympics. "I've always been driven," he would confide to a magazine writer years later. "From the time I was a kid, I always desperately wanted to work and make my own money in order to show myself I was somebody. I didn't think I was anybody, and work and money gave me a good feeling about myself. So I always had some kind of job."

Offered track and field scholarships from colleges across the country, Eugene chose the University of Southern California figuring he would have 365 days a year of warm weather in which to practice throwing the javelin. He also remembered his ill-fated California vacation when, at age ten, he'd almost drowned saving his mother from a similar fate. Even then, under those conditions, he had liked the sunshine, the ocean, and the balmy weather. Besides, USC had one of the best college track and field departments in the nation.

Although he had been officially accepted by the university, Eugene still could not believe he was finally on his way to college. He had made an eight-year plan for himself, based on what he would do as a championship javelin thrower, a plan that included a trip to the Olympics. But before he could graduate high school, there was the not-so-little matter of school detention slips. Having spent most of his two years as a sophomore ditching school and raising hell, Eugene had amassed an amazing number of detention hours for various infractions of school rules. In fact, it is rumored in Collingswood that, to this day, Eugene Orowitz holds the record number of forty-five-minute detentions in the history of Collingswood High.

"Actually," recalled his former physical education teacher, Bill Diemer, "it was remarkable that Eugene even graduated. He was an immense overachiever and probably very smart, but he was a rebellious kid and got into a lot of trouble. Plus his grades weren't that great. I really think it was due to Maurey Dickinson that Eugene stayed in school. Maurey was his mentor. He's the one that got him interested in the javelin. I think Eugene stayed around mostly for the track and the championships, things like that."

Whatever the cause behind Eugene's graduation, the fact was that before he could receive his high school diploma, he was forced by the school principal, Mr. Orlinger, to make up somewhere between two hundred and three hundred hours of detention slips.

"There was a wooden bench outside the school," recalled a former classmate, "and Orlinger made Eugene sit on that bench until the middle of July, making up his detention time, even though school officially ended in early June. It was something that everybody talked about then; and, of course, after Eugene became Michael Landon, they continued to talk about it."

While Eugene was busy killing detention time on the high school bench, Eli and Peggy Orowitz were busy getting ready to move to California. Eli wanted to return to his first love, publicity, and Peggy wanted her first love, daughter Evelyn, to become a movie star, an actress of the first magnitude. Since Eugene was going to be attending USC, it seemed to his parents that the occasion was perfect to bid farewell to New Jersey.

By the time Eugene had fulfilled his obligation to Collingswood High and had his high school diploma in hand, the family was in the midst of selling their home. A neighbor had agreed to purchase most of their furniture, and the plan was for Eli to accompany Eugene to Los Angeles, where he would get the boy settled in college and find suitable living accommodations, as well as a job. Peggy and Evelyn would follow after the sale of the house was final.

It was the early fifties and the world was still young. Elvis Presley was a singing truck driver yet to be discovered. Bobby sox and saddle shoes were all the rage. Drive-in movies had begun pulling people out of the movie houses and into the night air. And every member of the Orowitz household was elated, filled with their personal dreams of success.

Eugene was so excited about starting his life anew that he didn't lose a wink of sleep over selling his favorite possession — an aged Mercury convertible which, because it lacked a roof, would fill up with water every time it rained. Ugey, however, was unperturbed by the car's perpetual musty odor. After each torrential downpour, he'd simply pull up the carpets and let the water drain out of the holes he had kicked in the floorboards.

"It was the moment I'd dreamed of for as far back as I could remember," he explained years later. "Freedom. I wanted to be out on my own and in control of my own life. I wanted to be away from my family and out from under their control. It was that dream of being on my own that had helped me survive childhood."

With the money he had saved from his part-time jobs, plus the pittance he received for his car, Eugene and his father set out for California. His 1954 record as a javelin thrower was his passport out of Collingswood, his ticket for that long-awaited flight from his mother and all the misery he had endured throughout his childhood. He was a young man with a dream. He was going to be somebody, somebody important, somebody nobody could ever kick around again. Eugene Ugey Orowitz had taken over the reins of his life. He was in control now and he was going to stay in control.

Once in California, Eugene quickly enrolled at USC, and signed up as a major in speech and drama. Even though his older sister, Evelyn, was considered to be the promising thespian in the family, Eugene had always been secretly interested in acting. It was an interest that had begun when, at fourteen, he had played a Japanese houseboy in a Collingswood high school play. It had been only a tiny role, but it had gotten Ugey thinking about the possibilities. After all, Hollywood was practically under his nose. With his newly acquired confidence, he was convinced that acting just might be the right route for him to follow — after winning the Olympics competition, of course. Fate, however, has an odd way of sometimes short-circuiting even the best laid plans, often shattering dreams in the process.

In the fifties, crew cuts were the required cut for young men. It may have been the era of The Beat Generation, but even Jack Kerouac had closely cropped hair. Thus his teammates ridiculed him about his long hair and slight physique.

"I looked like Supermouse," he later laughed, "and the athletic department didn't know what to do with me. So they put me in a fraternity house, where I was a total misfit. Since they could hardly believe this was the javelin thrower they'd offered a scholarship, they tried me out, matching me against a big fellow, who must have been about six feet five. I outthrew him, and got my scholarship, and it drove the guy crazy."

Convinced that the length of his hair was somehow mystically tied into the distance he could throw a javelin, Eugene chose to ignore the taunts of his teammates. Shrugging off their constant jibes, he retreated into his own world. As a result, he found himself even more an outsider and an object of derision. Unfortunately, Eugene failed to realize just how big a threat he somehow posed to his close-cropped teammates who, unbeknown to him, had determined that with or without his cooperation, Eugene would become one of them in appearance, as well as in spirit.

Eugene showed up for field practice one afternoon and was immediately jumped by a group of his fellow athletes. While several of them held him down, the others laughingly lopped off half his hair. The result was a half crew cut, which then had to be finished by a barber. It was a chilling experience and one that he never forgot. Not only had he again found himself under the abusive control of others, he had been helpless to save what, at that point, had been his most priceless possession.

"I'd only been at USC four weeks when these guys held me down, shaved my head, and put some Atomic Balm on my scrotum," he would recall almost forty years later, with a shudder.

The following day, sporting his new crew cut, Eugene went back to the playing field to test his throwing powers, but the magic was gone. He continued throwing the javelin for hours, praying it would come back. But it didn't. Instead, he tore his shoulder ligaments and forever shattered his dream of being an Olympic contender. More importantly, since he couldn't perform on the playing field he couldn't live up to the terms of his scholarship.

If California had proven to be a disastrous experience for Eugene, it also proved to be devastating for his father who, like his son, had pinned his hopes for a new, successful life on the move.

Prior to leaving Collingswood, Eli had gotten in touch with former show business contacts, alerting them to his upcoming move to Los Angeles. Since he had been the head of publicity for RKO Radio Pictures in New York, he was certain he would have no difficulty whatsoever in landing a job. One of Eli's first job interviews was with several people he had worked for at RKO, who were now ensconced in positions of power at Paramount Studios.

With Eugene driving, the two pulled up to the studio gates on Melrose Avenue and Eli got out. "Wait here," he said, over his shoulder. "I'll be back in a minute to tell you where to park. Then we'll go on in."

Eugene was excited at the prospect of going on the huge Paramount lot and was hoping to get a tour, possibly even a glimpse of a star or two. He was so busy daydreaming, he didn't realize that a minute had turned into almost a half hour. Suddenly Eli returned and it was obvious that something was terribly wrong. His face was ashen, his shoulders were stooped and he looked twenty years older than he had a half hour before. The men he had thought were his friends, his ticket back into motion pictures, were all too busy to see him. He hadn't even been able to gain entrance to the lot. It was a humiliating experience for both father and son, something neither of them ever forgot . . . or forgave.

"The man had spent a lifetime working hard for people, worrying whether he was doing the best job, worrying whether people liked him, worrying whether he was doing all he could do," Michael would tell listeners years later. "And they wouldn't even talk to him. They just turned him away. My dad aged twenty years in that one half hour. His whole world fell apart."

In the few minutes it took for Eugene to understand what had happened to his father, he made a purposeful decision, a decision he would stick with for the rest of his life. Looking at his father, slumped in the passenger's seat, humiliated and defeated after years of dedicated hard work, Eugene Orowitz swore that no matter what, he was never going to owe anybody a favor.

"I wasn't going to expect anything from anybody that had to do with business," he explained to an interviewer more than thirty years later, "and I wasn't going to worry about somebody's friendship if it affected what I did for a living. Unlike my father," he added, "I wasn't going to take any garbage from anybody."

Unable to pay for USC without a scholarship, Eugene quit school in the middle of his freshman year. He took a job unloading freight cars, not only to make money, but to keep himself physically fit. Unlike his father, Eugene was not a beaten man. He was a new man with a new dream. As soon as he could afford it, he was going to enroll at UCLA and then "kick the crap out of USC in the javelin throw."

Luckily for Eugene, this was a dream he also failed to turn into a reality. He never enrolled at UCLA. In fact, he never returned to college. Instead he worked at a series of menial jobs and began focusing his energy on trying to break into acting. He was still a "nobody" but he was no longer on the path to "nowhere." He had a destination. He just didn't know if he was ever going to arrive there.

Three

The year following his departure from USC was a rough one for Eugene. Even though his hair had finally grown back, there wasn't much magic in his life. He was still a blue-collar worker who, having quit unloading freight cars, was still a nobody working in a ribbon factory. Living in a small apartment, barely able to make ends meet, he was making just enough money to pay his rent, put gas in his car, and food in his stomach. He didn't have to worry about saving money for a date because he rarely dated. One time he had gone out on a first date, but when the girl's friends saw the long-haired, strange-looking young man she was with, they had passed her a note expressing their worry: "Be careful." Eugene never saw her again.

One day, a coworker at the factory asked Eugene if he'd help him on a project. The fellow was a budding actor and needed someone to play opposite him in a scene for an audition.

"It was a scene from *Home of the Brave*," Landon would later tell interviewers, adding, "He gave me the sad part because he didn't want to cry." Eugene rehearsed with the guy and then joined him for the reading at Warner Bros. The pair did the scene, with Eugene crying up a storm and receiving kudos (but no offer of work) from the casting agent holding the audition. Nevertheless, Eugene decided perhaps acting really *was* his destination.

Hoping to be discovered, he took a job at a gas station directly across the street from Warner Bros. Since a lot of the studio executives had their cars serviced there, Eugene figured this was as good a place as any to gain exposure. And he was right. In true Hollywood fashion, he was "discovered" by a Warner executive who, taken by his dark good looks and his effervescent smile, suggested he join the studio's acting school. He joined the next day, and spent the following months developing his acting skills. One of his classmates was another aspiring actor, Jim Bumgarner, who also would find fame and riches as a TV superstar after changing his name to James Garner.

While attending the studio school and auditioning for roles, Landon worked as a salesman, selling blankets door-to-door. It was, he realized later, an invaluable experience because it taught him to communicate with all kinds of people.

"You can talk to anybody if you can sell door-to-door," he would later explain. "You really learn to read people. After that, if I was reading for a casting director who I knew could be intimidated, at some point I would reach across the desk, drag him over, and scream my lines at him. The reaction was always the same. He'd say, 'Well, he's not quite right for the part, but the kid has so much *emotion.*' And I'd get the part."

It was during the time, in 1956, that Michael met Dodie Fraser, a widow with a seven-year-old son, Mark. A legal secretary who had been widowed when her husband was killed in an automobile accident, Dodie was twenty-six, almost seven years older than the nineteen-year-old Eugene. Nevertheless, the two began dating and the romance became serious. Eugene was drawn to Dodie's warmth, her motherly instincts, her ability to nurture without being controlling, and he liked the way she treated her son. She was the kind of mother he had always wanted his mother to be: Kind and understanding.

The two became engaged, but as the wedding date grew near, Eugene began to have second thoughts about the marriage. He had begun to realize that he and Dodie actually had nothing in common, other than their love for her son, Mark.

"The day before the wedding, I told her I wanted to back out," Michael later confessed. "She said she understood but that I would have to explain it to Mark. I loved that boy and he loved me. I just couldn't hurt him. He was like me as a kid. Lonely. So we went ahead with the wedding."

And what a wedding day it turned out to be!

The ceremony, which would be the only church wedding Michael would ever have, was scheduled for the afternoon. Since his mother was distraught about his marriage and was refusing to attend the wedding, Eugene decided to visit his parents on his way to the church in an attempt to persuade his mother to change her mind. The visit turned out to be a major mistake.

"When it was time to leave for the church," he would later recall, "my mother pulled a knife on me. So I called the police. 'I don't want to hit her,' I told them, 'but I don't want to get stabbed, either.' So the cops came over to the house, and this real nice one said, 'Now, mother, your son's of age. You know he can leave.' To which my mother replied, 'He's mentally ill and I'm having him committed.' And she called the state mental hospital!"

Eugene left with the police and the wedding went off without any further complications, but neither Peggy or Eli Orowitz attended the ceremony. After that, Michael distanced himself from his mother, and after the death of his father, he saw her less than half a dozen times until her death in 1981.

Although Eugene had been slowly making his way into motion pictures, appearing on live television dramas such as "Playhouse 90" and "Studio One," and in forgettable "B" films, life continued to be a struggle. He even embarked on a short-lived singing career, recording "Gimme a Little Kiss, Will Ya, Huh?" and then touring briefly with Jerry Lee Lewis.

Dodie's paycheck as a legal secretary made her the basic breadwinner of the family, while Eugene worked at odd jobs and auditioned for every role he thought he might stand a chance of winning. He even took to the stage, garnering an impressive review for his work in a West Coast production of *Tea and Sympathy*.

By this time he had changed his name. Eugene Orowitz simply wasn't marquee material. Looking in the telephone book, he had first chosen the moniker Michael Lane. Then when a search of the Screen Actor's Guild roster showed a Michael Lane was already registered, Eugene Orowitz became Michael Landon. And not a moment too soon. His career was beginning to build momentum. He had a small role in the film *God's Little Acre,* and then he landed his first starring role.

Having spent two years waiting for a break,

Michael failed to recognize it when it finally arrived. No one would have suspected that a low-budget horror flick with the title *I Was a Teenage Werewolf* would be the vehicle to offer any real screen success. But it was. Produced by Herman Cohen, the 1957 film became an overnight sensation and remains a cult classic today. He had accepted the title role because he needed the money and because the lead role in a film, any film, could only help his career. He was right. *Werewolf* earned Landon instant recognition and marked his first giant step forward in an acting career that ultimately would make him a multimillionaire and a major TV star.

The following year, 1958, Michael landed small roles in films such as "High School Confidential" and "God's Little Acre." He also had the lead in another low-budget film, a western titled *The Legend of Tom Dooley*. Although the film was forgettable, the song of the same title became a major Top 40 hit and the musical launching pad for the folksinging threesome who recorded it, the Kingston Trio. Michael, on the other hand, had little to gain from the film other than money and another credit beneath his name, or so he thought.

It was the second day of rehearsals for *Tom Dooley* and Michael was in the midst of going over dialogue when he received a frantic telephone call from Dodie: His father had died. After his humiliating experience at Paramount studios, when he realized his career as a publicist was finished, Eli Orowitz had settled for the first job he could get . . . as the manager of a movie house on Vermont Avenue in the Los Feliz area of Hollywood. It wasn't a well-paying job, but it was a job.

A man of habit, Eli had lunch every day at approximately the same time at the same restaurant next door to the theater. "I'll try your soup of the day," he'd always say. Then, once it was served, he'd take a sip and say, "That's very good." One day, according to Michael, his father sipped the soup, said "That's very good," and dropped dead of a heart attack. "I hope that's the way I go," Michael told his listeners. "Fast, no pain, no suffering. Just the blink of an eye, like my dad. He never knew what hit him."

Eli's fatal heart attack was the first time Michael had experienced the death of a loved one; and although he'd known his father was not in the best of health, it still came as a shock. What was even more surprising to him was that he was actually grieving for his father, a man he'd known all of his life but who had been a virtual stranger. Although his mother and sister, Evelyn, were living in Los Angeles, the responsibility for the details of his father's burial service fell on Michael, who was grateful that he had become closer to Eli the year just prior to his death.

"I really never knew my father until about a year before he died because he moved in with me and lived out the last year of his life at my house," Michael once confided to several crew members, after telling them the story of Eli's death. "But at that point," he had added, "it was really too late for us to become close, like a father and son should be. Too much water had run under the proverbial bridge by then. I did learn that a lot of my father's pain, a lot of what he had kept inside all those years, were things he shouldn't have kept hidden. I learned a lot about his relationship with my mother whom he had stayed with all those miserable years just for the sake of my older sister and me. It was a tragedy that never should have happened."

Still stunned by Eli's death, Michael returned to continue shooting *Tom Dooley,* a film he later termed "one of the most disastrous jobs" he'd ever had. Whether it was the emotional trauma of losing his father, or just bad luck, Michael became accident-prone.

The first mishap, when he accidentally stabbed himself in the face with a knife, could have disfigured him and ruined a budding movie career. After that, the fact that he was shot in the face at close range by a gun filled with blanks, and later broke his foot, somehow seemed insignificant.

"I was cutting this guy off a horse and I didn't want to cut towards him because I was afraid I'd hurt him," Michael later recalled. "But the first time I went to cut the rope, the knife wouldn't cut through it. So the propman switched knives and gave me one of those big scout knives, the kind they used to carry in westerns, with a really sharp Wilkinson blade. I yelled the line of dialogue on cue and didn't even realize the blade had gone through the rope, because it had gone through it like a piece of butter. The next thing I knew, I was bleeding. I'd stabbed myself in the mouth!

"A Dr. Edelstein sewed my face up and did a hell of a good job on me, too. I went to a party two weeks later . . . there were quite a few other actors around my age at the party . . . the same ones I'd seen at auditions . . . and I've never seen such disappointment. It was written all over their faces. They'd heard about the accident and were betting I'd walk in looking like something out of *Frankenstein,*" he had laughed, adding, "They were really depressed I wasn't ruined."

The Legend of Tom Dooley may have been a disaster at the box office, as well as a personal disaster for Michael, but the film and its star caught the eye of producer David Dortort, who was looking for a handsome, young, virile actor to portray the youngest son of a man named Pa Cartwright in an hour-long television western series he had created for NBC. The show was titled "Bonanza."

Michael was afraid to get too excited about the possibility of starring in a television series, even if his agent *was* telling him it was a sure thing. He'd had "sure things" before and they'd usually come to nothing. This time, he confided to Dodie, he would believe it was a sure thing *only* after he'd signed the contract and the check was not just in the mail, it was in the bank.

He was prepared for anything, but when he learned that he had been cast in the role of "Little Joe," by his own admission he "almost fainted." Michael Landon had become financially stable. Not only was he steadily employed, he was bringing in a hefty five hundred dollars a week. As he would later explain to interviewers: "I didn't have any money in those days and when they came to me and said they would pay me every week, well, I know how those people that win the lottery must feel."

For Michael, the role of "Little Joe" would prove to be a heady fourteen-year gallop from rags to riches. "When it ended it was very painful for everybody," Michael would confess, "it really was."

Four

Set during the Civil War years, "Bonanza" starred Lorne Greene as Pa Cartwright, the patriarchal owner of the Ponderosa, a 1,000-square-mile ranch not far from Virginia City, Nevada, whose three sons were portrayed by Pernell Roberts, Dan Blocker, and of course, Michael Landon.

In what turned out to be a case of perfect casting, Pernell landed the role of Pa's oldest son, Adam, who always wore black and seemed to be in a perpetual black mood. Dan Blocker portrayed Hoss, a kindly, gentle bear of a man whose simple mind and sunny disposition provided a nice balance to the brooding Adam. And Michael played "Little Joe," the youngest, most handsome, and the most impetuous of Pa's three boys. The other regular cast member was Victor Sen Yung, who played the Cartwright family's faithful, often comic houseboy, Hop Sing.

With a soaring theme song from the musical pen of David Rose, "Bonanza" debuted on the NBC network on September 12, 1959. It had the distinction of being the first western television series ever to be televised in color. Other than that, the series was only moderately successful during its first two seasons, a situation created in large part because it was pitted against CBS's hit drama "Perry Mason."

Several years after "Bonanza" bit the dust, Lorne Greene admitted that he had been surprised when the series pilot sold. "It was one of the worst pilots ever made," he said, "but the color was marvelous. I suspect the man who bought the show, bought it for its marvelous color, not for its marvelous content." Greene was most probably right. Had "Bonanza" not been shot in color, it probably wouldn't have lasted longer than a season or two. But those were the early days of color and RCA, which owned NBC, was anxious to sell color TV sets. So the show languished on Saturday nights, selling color television sets but never attaining any great popularity with the viewing public.

Then, in a programming move which turned out to be brilliant in retrospect, the network moved the show to Sunday evenings. At the same time, Dortort and NBC also toned down Pa's character, switching him from a "fire and brimstone, stop that fighting!" kind of guy to a gentler, more understanding fellow. As a result of these changes, "Bonanza" became one of the biggest television hits of the sixties.

Although the show did not deal in great themes, grand passions, of visual flamboyance, the series nevertheless held the attention of viewers. "Bonanza" ranked number one in the Nielsen ratings for three consecutive seasons, and in the Nielsen Top Ten for a decade. it managed to kill off such TV rivals as Judy Garland, Garry Moore, and the Smothers Brothers in the process. Supposedly the show was so popular that then-President Lyndon Johnson even had a speech rescheduled so that it would not be in competition with "Bonanza."

A low-key show, with only a minimum of violence, "Bonanza" offered viewers sixty minutes of traditional morality, family values, and just enough action to keep the story moving. The hour always began the same, with the four actors riding toward the camera through a hole in a burning map of Nevada. And the scripts were always the same: One of the well-meaning Cartwright siblings would get into trouble, only to be rescued by an amazing combination of good fortune, virtue, and the fatherly ministrations of Lorne Greene. There would always be a crisis and then Pa Cartwright and his sons would race out of their ranch house, jump on their steeds, and be off to remedy the situation, whatever it was.

"It was a good thing we weren't miked for those scenes in which the four of us Cartwrights would come running out of the house, mount our horses, and ride away," Michael laughingly recounted, "because, as far as I was concerned, Lorne's horse was called, 'Whoa, you son of a bitch.' He'd only been on a horse once before in his life and didn't know how to ride any better than I did, although you would have thought he was a veteran of the Royal Canadian Mounted Police until the first week of shooting. Then the truth came out. Dan was the best rider of the four of us, although actually, I don't know if Pernell Roberts was a good horseman or not. He didn't speak to me, so I didn't speak to him."

Another of Michael's favorite horse stories involved the time when, early in the series, the stars were invited to participate in the annual Pasadena Rose Bowl Parade. "We were 75th in line and there must have been 4,000 horses and 18,000 drums ahead of us," Michael said laughing, "when all of a sudden our horses took off and we completed the entire route in about four minutes. Blocker was cursing a blue streak. I was hanging on for dear life. Pernell's lips were pursed more than usual. And Lorne was waving to the crowd with a great flourish as he raced by."

Hal "Bubba" Burton, who was Landon's

stunt double for eighteen years, recalled the early days of "Bonanza," when Greene and Blocker, along with Landon and other guys from the crew, would play cards, toss horseshoes, throw rocks and darts to while away their time between scenes. "It was one big family," he said. "Mike was very competitive, but he was probably the most unstar-like guy I ever met. He liked being just one of the guys. He liked to play pool and he loved to eat. Boy, for a little guy, could Mike eat. I once saw him down three giant-size prime ribs at one meal. And it wasn't unusual for us to go out and have a half dozen eggs and three steaks for breakfast. But he kept in shape. He was always working out. He was always in great shape."

Despite the foursome's lack of riding expertise and the predictable scripts, the show's format worked. "Bonanza" remained on the air for fourteen successful years, making each of its stars a multimillionaire, with the exception of Pernell Roberts, who departed in 1966 after having spent most of his six years voicing a long litany of complaints about the show. According to Roberts, the show was sexist. Ben Cartwright resembled a South American dictator, and his grown sons were so retarded they had to ask his permission to leave the Ponderosa. The list went on and on.

Not surprisingly, there were no tears shed when Roberts finally followed through on his continuous threat to quit and departed. The only person in the series who seemed sad to see him go was his TV father, Lorne Greene, who urged the headstrong actor not to be "a damn fool."

"Take their money and buy your own theater," Greene advised, ponting out, "Then you can hire Tennessee Williams to write a play just for you."

But Roberts wasn't listening, not even to Pa Cartwright. " 'Bonanza' is bad literature," he explained, "and I am tired of trying to hide that fact. My being a part of this show is like asking Isaac Stern to sit in with Lawrence Welk."

With that, Roberts rode off into the sunset, only to reappear on the television horizon twenty years later as the star of the CBS series "Trapper John, M.D." He had spent the intervening years struggling to support himself with summer tours and starring roles in dinner theaters. Having ruined his reputation in Hollywood as a "troublemaker," he had found few doors open to him in the realm of television and motion pictures. At one point, hurting for money, the "Isaac Stern" of the acting profession had even appeared in television commercials.

"After I left, the show went through the ceiling and made everyone millionaires, so I lost a lot of money by leaving. Still," he said years later, "I have no regrets. Money just doesn't run my life."

"Pernell didn't like the show and would let

you know it," Michael later explained, "but he rarely cared to do much about improving it. To say a show stinks doesn't make it better. I would tell the director 'This is a piece of crap.' But I wasn't like Pernell. His attitude was negative. I'd give reasons.

"After he left we took one leaf out of the dining room table and we all made money because we split the take three ways instead of four."

The year after Roberts departed, Dortort hired David Canary to portray a ranch hand named Candy. Canary appeared in the role from 1967 through 1970, then returned for the show's last season in 1972.

Unlike Roberts, Michael saw tremendous potential, as well as fame and riches, to be gleaned from his role of "Little Joe." He may have spent most of the first years uttering "Yes, Pa," to Lorne Greene, but by the third year on the series, he had begun to want more out of his career than simply appearing before the camera. He began to realize that the power in television, as well as in motion pictures, rested in the hands of the producer and the director. Of course, if you could write and then star in your own material you would become a quadruple threat, commandeering four times as much money, as well as all the control. And control, not money, had always been extremely important to Michael.

As a producer, Michael would have total control of a show. As a director, he would have complete power over the set. As a writer he would have the power to control the tone and subject matter of the series. And as the star of the series, he would have the fame, the accolades, the recognition he needed to continue proving to himself that he was somebody.

So while most of Hollywood dismissed him as just another pretty face, Landon was slowly paving the path for an illustrious future by experimenting with cinematography and writing.

"The producers were often so busy on 'Bonanza' they would send us scripts with scenes without dialogue," he explained. "So I started writing dialogue for those missing two-minute scenes. I tried to inject some humor into them, like having Dan Blocker do something silly, like throw me out the window, at the end of a scene. It was fun, and it added something special to the show."

A few years later, when "Bonanza" was on the verge of shutting down production for a week while the producers looked for new scripts, Landon seized the moment. He sat on his livingroom floor and, using the coffee table as a desk, over the weekend wrote a full episode of the show in longhand on yellow legal pads.

"Actually, I didn't want to lose three weeks' salary," Michael joked, "so I went home and wrote the script. It wasn't brilliant, but I brought it in on Monday and we started shooting it on Wednesday."

Titled *The Gamble,* the episode turned out to

be a ratings success, and Michael was on his way to establishing himself as a force with which to be reckoned. To make sure that he didn't lose his way along the path, Michael hired Jay Bernstein, a leading Hollywood publicist at the time, to insure that Hollywood power brokers knew there was more to Michael than just another handsome face. Bernstein did his job well. Landon received a lot of attention in both *The Hollywood Reporter* and *Daily Variety,* the two trade publications devotedly read by members of the TV and film industry, as well as from the general press. *The Gamble* garnered rave reviews, and everyone from New York to Los Angeles knew that "Little Joe" had written the script and planned to write more scripts in the future.

"Even then he knew what he wanted and where he would be now," Bernstein recently recalled. "Mike is strong-willed and strong-principled and I respect him for that. He wanted to do things his way. He told me, 'Look, I don't want any personal publicity. If I'm writing or directing something, I want you to publicize that. I want people to see that.' But he did have 'The Look,' " Bernstein added. "He could have been a major star. He could have been the next Cary Grant, but he just wasn't interested. He was more interested in being behind the camera than in front of it. I always thought that was a shame, but like I said, Michael always knew what he wanted."

What Michael wanted, of course, is what Michael had always wanted: Power. The millions of dollars he would ultimately earn from his writing, directing, producing, and acting were only by-products of his drive to become a "player." He was a man on the move, filled with nervous energy, unable to sleep more than four or five hours a night. He was uptight, nervous, and compelled not to let life somehow pass him by.

Years later, just after he turned fifty, Landon would reflect on how driven he was in these early days. "I'm not as hard on myself as I used to be," he confided. "I used to worry all the time about what I wrote and directed. I used to chew my tongue until it was raw—one side, then the other."

But in the "Bonanza" days, Michael was flying through life as though he were being chased by a thousand devils, and perhaps he was.

"It's really amazing how fast he could write," a friend dating back to Landon's "Bonanza" days confided, adding, "The problem was he's left-handed and he wrote so quickly, nobody except his secretary could read it."

Another close friend not only admires Landon's writing acumen, he admires the emotion Landon could pour literally and figuratively onto a written page. "I've actually seen water spots on the pages of a script he'd have been up most of the night writing," he said. "You see, Mike is very emotional. It would be a sad story and

61

he'd apparently start crying, and those spots were where his tears had fallen onto the page. He wrote close to the edge of his emotions."

Bill Kiley, an NBC publicist who worked with Landon on all three of his network series, agrees with that assessment. "Michael's emotions *were* close to the surface. There was a lot of pain in Michael, a lot of unresolved hurt and anger. I remember several times when I would be out on the set and I'd see Michael standing off camera, telling a raunchy joke to some of the crew. Then he'd step in front of the camera to do a heavy dramatic scene, and the minute the director yelled 'Action,' Michael would cry on cue.

"Well, I thought this was one of the more amazing things I'd ever seen. So one day I asked him, 'How can you do that?' He said, 'It's simple. I just remember my dad and what this town did to him.' "

"Mike was the kind of guy who, even though he was a big star, could still go sit under a tree, put his feet up and just bullshit," Bill Kiley recalled. "He was as unspoiled an actor as you'll ever find. He also was a great practical joker," Kiley added, recounting the time Landon had seen Burton eating his second or third ice cream cone.

"You're getting fat, Bubba," Landon said as he passed by several times, and Burton was still devouring the ice cream. Then, Landon got an idea. He went to the wardrobe man and had him start taking in Burton's costume a half inch a week for almost six weeks. By the end of the third week, Burton was on a full-fledged diet, convinced he was literally eating himself out of a job.

"He was a happy-go-lucky, likable goof-off in the early days of 'Bonanza' and, of course, he was handsome as hell. But Mike tired very quickly of the money and fame. He wanted to write and direct and that's when he really blossomed. By the time 'Little House' went on the air he was acting, directing and writing. He really knew family television. In my mind, he was the Walt Disney of television."

Five

During his early years on "Bonanza" Michael began supplementing his income by making personal appearances at rodeos across the country. He would leave the set as soon as shooting had wrapped up on Friday, grab a plane for whatever town he was scheduled to appear in that weekend, do the rodeo, then jump on a plane Sunday and be back at work Monday morning. In recalling that period of his life, Michael said that one of his "most humbling" experiences occurred on his first night of personal appearances as a star of "Bonanza."

"I took everyone's advice," he explained, "and did sophisticated songs and jokes, instead of western stuff representative of the series. Well, the audience, which was in bowling shirts and cowboy boots, started booing and shifting around in their seats. It was very uncomfortable being out there on that stage. After that, I went back to my old state-fair act."

Michael continued working his unrelenting seven-day work schedule, traveling the rodeo and fair circuit on the weekends, until the frenetic pace finally got to him. Exhausted, he collapsed on a plane on his way back to Los Angeles.

"My body was on overload in those days," he explained to the press, adding: "When you're young, your body is strong and will keep going. But the mind won't. What happens is the mind gets so exhausted and so tired it says, 'I'm going to do the best thing I can for you: I am going to turn off.' And it does. You just lose control of everything. It looked like I was having an epileptic attack, a grand mal seizure. It was very bad and scared the hell out of everybody on the plane." What Michael neglected to reveal, however, was that he was drinking heavily and popping an amazing number of amphetamines on a daily basis just to keep going. He was miserable . . . and miserable to be around, both on the "Bonanza" set and at home.

Michael was twenty-two years old when he filmed the "Bonanza" pilot. When the show became a huge hit, he had a difficult time adjusting to his newly acquired star status. "It was a shock," he would later admit. "All of a sudden, I was Don Juan, with women going crazy, screaming, and pushing police cars over. I was terrified because it had happened, everything that I'd dreamed about had happened, and I was afraid it would end. I had a hard time handling it."

Michael always had a difficult time trusting anyone outside of his carefully picked circle of friends. So when stardom struck and he was suddenly in demand by fan magazines, effusive directors, and swarms of beautiful women suggesting they were at his beck and call, Landon became even more distrustful of Hollywood types.

"I didn't know who they really wanted to see," he would later confide, "me or the star. And a lot of people wanted something from me. And they expected me to give it to them. Business people, the press, everybody. But I remembered my father, and I wasn't going to fall into that trap."

As hotheaded off the screen as he was in his "Little Joe" character, Landon would invariably find himself in a fistfight during one of his weekend appearances. "Everyone wanted to say they punched out a Cartwright," he complained. He was happy to give them the chance to try.

Meanwhile, back on the "Bonanza" set, he became legendary for his temper tantrums and unbridled ego; and within the industry, he gained the reputation of being an arrogant, nasty, know-it-all, who had more luck than talent, someone who would disappear in a cloud of dust once "Bonanza" bit the dust.

It was then that Lorne Greene stepped in, becoming Michael's surrogate father in real life, as well as his on-screen "Pa."

"When I first met Mike," Green would recall, "he was a kid. His real father had died a year or two before 'Bonanza' started and we just sort of drifted together. If he had a problem, he would come to me and say, 'Lorne, can I have dinner with you tonight at your house?' I'd say 'sure' and after dinner we would talk. I think that meant a lot to him."

With fatherly patience and understanding, Greene listened to Michael discuss his unhappiness with his life, especially his marriage. Greene was supportive and concerned about Michael, who seemed hell-bent on self-destruction, and urged him to slow down with his drinking.

"I did drink an awful lot during 'Bonanza,' " Michael would later confess to a friend. "I tried to depend on work for my happiness, and after work I would head for the nearest bar. I just didn't want to go home. I was never an alcoholic, but there was hardly a night I didn't get plastered.

"I was unhappy and I'd do dumb things. I wanted to be upset about something. I'd turn into a basket case if I had finished work and the studio didn't have a car waiting to take me away immediately. My attitude was that everything should be my way. I wanted to have arguments. I wanted to pick fights with people. So I'd throw a tantrum. I'd take out my unhappiness on my coworkers," he later admitted.

"Right in the middle of a planned and rehearsed fight scene, for instance, I'd kick in and do it for real. I'd scream a profanity in the middle of filming . . . not even realizing it at the time. One time I was doing a fight with a stunt man and had no idea I was doing it for real. I'd bulldogged him off a horse and we rolled off a hill. He looked at me with the strangest look, but I ran at him and we continued the fight. Afterwards, he told me he thought I was going to kill him. I was a real pain in the ass."

It wasn't just alcohol that was causing his angry outbursts, however. Michael had become hooked on amphetamines, thanks to a physician who prescribed Miltown, an addictive relaxant, to treat his growing anxiety. At the height of his addiction, he was popping anywhere from twenty to thirty pills a day and could not function without them. For a normal person, a single dose of twenty tablets would probably result in a fatal overdose. However, for someone addicted to the drug, almost limitless amounts of the pill can be tolerated if the addiction develops over a period of time.

"I was turning into a marshmallow," he admitted years later. "I couldn't do anything without getting a headache. It was so bad that I could hear the blood splashing inside my head. And in the morning when the alarm would go off, I couldn't sit up without getting a migraine. I would have to reach over to the nightstand, take three or four Miltowns with a glass of water, then lie there and wait for them to take effect so that I could get up and go out to work."

Michael had thought that the joy he'd found in his work would be enough to sustain him. What he was discovering was that it wasn't. He was unhappy at home and didn't want to be there. Yet he felt an obligation to Dodie, and to Mark and Josh, the infant sons they'd adopted shortly after their marriage. He was making more money than he'd ever imagined in his wildest dreams. Yet he was living beyond his means and having to work those weekend rodeos, turning his life into a grinding seven-day schedule, just to keep up. More importantly, he was still filled with unresolved anger toward his mother and the miserable childhood he somehow could not seem to escape. He had trapped himself in a marital corner that had become as emotionally distressing as the home life he had endured as a youth growing up in Collingswood.

"I had thought that being a star was going to make me happy, but there is absolutely no link between success and happiness. I learned that the hard way," he revealed years later.

Realizing he and his marriage had both become intolerable, Michael finally summoned up enough courage to ask Dodie for a divorce. It was an extremely difficult step for Michael to take, but having grown up in a dysfunctional family, he knew that to remain in an unhappy marriage simply for the sake of the children, in this case Mark and Josh, was worse than divorce. "I didn't want to go through life as my parents did, never laughing or really having fun," he later explained to friends.

Michael and Dodie were amicably divorced in 1962 after almost six years of marriage. "We were both good people, it's just that we didn't have anything in common," was Michael's explanation to the press.

Dodie received custody of Mark and Josh, and Michael received his freedom, as well as unlimited visiting rights with the boys. Since the legal papers had never been signed, it was decided that Jason, an infant the couple had adopted only the year before, would be returned to the adoption agency, rather than become part of a divided family. It was a decision that would come back to haunt Michael almost thirty years later when, in the midst of his battle against pancreatic cancer, the story of Jason became front page tabloid news.

In 1962, however, Michael's mind was not on what the press might print about him thirty years into the future. His mind was on his career and a beautiful twenty-six-year-old model, Marjorie Lynn Noe, whom he had been secretly dating while still married to Dodie.

Six

A divorcée with a young daughter, Cheryl, Lynn was a fairly successful model who worked as an extra in movies and television to support herself between modeling assignments. The couple met on the set of "Bonanza" when Lynn was hired for a day's work in a small-bit scene. It had been love at first sight, she would later admit, even though at first she didn't know who he was.

"There was a very strong physical pull," Lynn recalled, adding, "I decided not to go home, and that was not my style — to hang around the set. I had changed from my western costume into my own clothes and he came over and started talking. When the shooting was over he asked me for a drink. He was married at the time, but he had his own life, even though he was still living with his first wife.

"The electricity between us was very strong, but in my mind he was still married, so I decided to keep seeing him but to continue with my own life," she continued, "to see other men. I never wanted to be the other woman. I knew I loved him, but I was unsure. He was full of conflict and he was drinking too much. He often says that if he hadn't met me he might have had a drinking problem."

According to Lynn, when she would come home with a date she'd see Michael's car, supposedly hidden, parked outside her apartment building. "So," she later laughed, "I would invite my date in, even if I had to run around the room for thirty minutes to keep him there. I had no intention of pressuring Michael, even though the truth is, I would have married him a week after I met him. I never gave him an ultimatum. I just left town, deliberately. I accepted a modeling assignment in New York and worked there for three weeks. When I came back, he was ready to change his life and proceeded to get a divorce."

By that time, Michael was totally in love with Lynn. "She was in an L & M commercial and I used to just keep on flipping the dial, hoping to see her," he would later laughingly recall. It was the first time he'd ever really loved another human being, and the first time he had ever felt truly loved. As a result, he stopped spending his off-hours in bars. Instead he spent all of his time away from the "Bonanza" set with Lynn. Their courtship was intense but it felt good to Michael. Finally, he believed, he'd met his soul mate, the right woman for him. He was giddy. He was happy. He was in love.

"What I discovered when I met Lynn was that I could be a very happy person. Before that, I didn't have faith that I would ever find someone to love. In fact, I believed I would find pleasure solely from pretending to be someone else. That's why I liked acting so much."

After that, Lynn and Michael met for dinner almost nightly, but they were so busy holding hands and talking, they rarely ate. Michael would later joke it was hunger, rather than lust, that finally got him to propose to Lynn: "We're starving to death," he told her. "Let's get married."

Lynn accepted the proposal and the two eloped to Mexico, where they were married in "some old building" by a minister who got his speech confused, asking her, "Do you like this man to be your wedded husband?"

Returning to Los Angeles, the couple set up housekeeping in a small apartment, along with Lynn's young daughter, Cheryl, whom Michael later adopted. Within a year Lynn gave birth to the couple's first child, a daughter whom they named Leslie, and the following year, Lynn gave birth to a boy, Michael Graham. When Lynn had a miscarriage a year or so later, Michael decided three children was plenty and had a vasectomy. Several years later, however, after seeing a couple playing with their new baby at a neighbor's pool party, he had the operation reversed. The couple soon had two more children, Shawna, and four years after her birth, Christopher.

After he married Lynn, Michael continued to drink, but not as heavily as he had in the past. With Lynn's help and fortitude, he totally stopped his dependency on prescription drugs. He was a new man.

"I became more positive after Lynn and I were married," he confessed, "and the things I enjoyed were simpler. Just being together was fun. I handled my temper better. I got along with people better. Now I don't have to make a stunt fight into a real fight to release my frustrations. Now I go home because that's where I can talk about the things that are bothering me."

Lynn and Michael were one of the happiest couples in Hollywood. They were the portrait of togetherness. Wherever Michael was, Lynn and the children were by his side, except when he was filming "Bonanza" and later, "Little House." It was what she wanted. It was what Michael wanted.

"Michael always made me feel secure," Lynn said. "I always traveled with him in those early days. He said, 'Come with me.' And I never refused. I didn't care if it was some county fair in Tall Town, Iowa. I knew we would find something fun out of it. So if other women were after him, I was there. But he never let women touch him, kiss him, he never compromised me. I always had dignity. Michael always said, 'I kiss children and old ladies.' He has always been a very thoughtful man. He has always taken the time to leave me phone numbers, even in the cutting room, where he could be reached. He is a very considerate man, either that or a very smart cookie."

"When I'm doing gigs — fairs, rodeos — where I sing my songs, tell my jokes, I take the whole family with me," Michael explained, adding, "Fairs and rodeos are a lot of fun, the money's great, and the whole thing is a walk in the park.

"It's not what people do when they're apart. By nature I'm a very jealous person and it's just better for me to have my wife around. She makes everything bearable. We can always go back to the room and have a cheeseburger and a chuckle about everything."

There is no question that Lynn Noe was one of the best things that ever happened to Michael Landon. She gave him love and security, and the desire to prove himself in constructive ways, rather than in the destructive ways he'd previously allowed to shape his life. Gone was the drinking. Abandoned was the hostility and the fights his anger had often encouraged. In their place was a more moderate Michael. He was filled with hope and overflowing with creative energy. He would keep Lynn up half the night discussing his plans for the future, his ideas for scripts, and his desire to become more than simply an actor. It was during the early years of his marriage to Lynn that Michael really began to flourish—as a human being and as a creative member of the television industry.

"I didn't have a lot of motivation, but when I met Lynn, I found I had someone who believed in me, who was supportive of me," he would later admit. "So I wanted her to be proud of me. If I hadn't met her, I don't think I would have done any of this," he concluded, referring to his writing and directing.

Of course, no marriage is perfect. One of Lynn's pet peeves was that Michael was often as much a child as his children. "He's not as disciplined with the children as I would like," she confided. "At dinner he fools around with them more than I would like. But that's Michael. He had a very unhappy childhood, so in some ways, he's a child himself. He's a very loving father and gives a lot of time to our children."

Michael also used to drive Lynn crazy, she said, because "he never remembers where he puts anything. I have to always pick up after him. He doesn't have a key to the house because within two days I'd have to have sixteen locks changed because he would have misplaced his key."

Michael, himself, would laugh at his forgetfulness. He had one credit card that he carried around in a back pocket of his jeans, but it was unusable. "Somebody finally gave me a credit-card holder, but my card was so bent and destroyed I couldn't even get it in the metal holder," he joked.

And then there was his temper.

"I have a terrible temper," Michael candidly

admitted, "and I do the most childish things imaginable when I lose it. Lynn hates to argue so she won't fight back, which of course infuriates me further. I'll do something like flip off the TV set and say, 'It's mine. If you can't argue with me you can't watch my television.' I make an utter fool out of myself and then I get mad about that.

"The worst is when you storm out the door and say, 'Okay. That's it. I'm leaving!' And you know she knows you'll be back in ten minutes because you've got no place to go and you don't want to leave in the first place.

"My wife," he had added, "is a beautiful, wise, and patient woman. I love my work and I'm delighted to be in a profession that pays so well for doing something that you enjoy. But my work is nothing compared to my wife and family. I can handle anything that comes up at work as long as I know everything is okay at home. No career achievement," he had concluded, "could mean as much as Lynn's love. I'd never been in love before I met her."

Seven

In May, 1972, Dan Blocker, who was only forty-three years old, died suddenly after what was supposed to be routine surgery. Four months later, after thirteen successful seasons, "Bonanza" was also on its way to the graveyard. The series had begun to lose ratings, so at the beginning of the 1972#73 fall season, NBC shifted it into a new time slot on Tuesday evenings. It was a fatal blow to the show.

Pitted against "Maude" on CBS, and the "ABC Movie of the Week," the series plummeted in the Nielsen ratings, dropping out of the Top Ten and into fortieth place by the first week of October, 1972. Then on Monday, November 6, 1972, Lawrence White, vice president of NBC programming, announced that the series would be replaced by yet another night of prime-time movies, effective January 23, 1973.

"We were on Sunday nights for eleven years and we knocked off all the competition thrown at us," Dortort said, adding, "I think we could have gone on four or five years more. We had broken out of the traditional clichés of the television western; we were telling stories about people with real problems."

In examining the causes behind the show's cancellation, Dortort felt Blocker's death had been a major blow. "I guess when you really get down to it," he said, "we just didn't have enough time to find a substitute for Dan. I know at the beginning it was Ben Cartwright who was the central character, but you know, after a few years Hoss became the foundation for the show, the central character, and you just don't find another Hoss."

Blocker's death devastated everyone, from the cast to the crew to the show's many fans. It was a particularly hard blow for Michael, who told a magazine writer: "We never thought we could die. We'd been shot, stabbed, kicked, run over by wagons. You begin to believe all that—then someone tells you your brother's dead. Whoa."

If Lorne had become his father figure, Dan had become like the brother Michael had never had. The three men had become extremely close, personally and professionally.

"Lorne was like our father," Michael once said, recalling how he and Dan would "play tricks" on Greene. "Once Dan and I were driving Lorne and his wife, Nancy, down a winding canyon road, and just as we started our descent, Dan, who was driving, yelled, 'Oh, my gosh, I don't have any brakes.'

"Well, Lorne and Nancy, who were in the backseat, believed us. They were so terrified, they ducked down on the floor behind the front seat, and they stayed there until we got to the bottom of the hill. Dan and I almost burst from holding in our laughter. Finally, when we got to the bottom of the hill, Dan sighed. 'Whew!' he said. 'We've got to get those brakes fixed.' Then we looked at each other, and at Lorne and Nancy getting up from the floor, and we couldn't keep from laughing."

Another of Michael's favorite stories about Lorne was the time when, toward the beginning of "Bonanza," he and Greene were making personal appearances together at rodeos all over the country.

"Lorne was supposed to sing the finale song, and just as we were about to go onstage I walked up to him, with a worried look on my face, and told him I'd just heard there was a sniper in the audience. Of course, there wasn't. It was just one of my pranks. Well, being the trouper that he was, Lorne wanted to please all the fans. So he bravely insisted on going onstage anyway. I can still see him, singing the finale, moving rapidly all around the stage, trying to avoid being an easy target for the madman in the audience. We had a lot of laughs about that for years afterward."

Years after Blocker's death, Michael would still speak nostalgically about his friendship with Dan and Lorne. "We had a close family feeling, and cared very much for each other. This all intensified

81

when Dan died suddenly in 1972. At that point Lorne and I began to appreciate each other more than ever. For me, Dan's death was like losing a brother."

By the time "Bonanza" was canceled, Michael had established himself as a writer and director, as well as an actor. So while he wasn't overjoyed that the golden goose had finally died, he was looking forward to going out on his own, establishing his own projects. While Michael was shocked and disgusted by the offhanded way NBC announced the show's cancellation, Lorne Greene was angered by the callous treatment of the network.

"They told us on Monday that we would quit shooting on Wednesday (November 8, 1972)," he angrily told a reporter. "After you've been on the air for fourteen years, even if you're a caretaker, you should get a month's notice. They felt they didn't have to do that because our contract said we got paid for that year, whether we did any shows or not. But that wasn't the point. The point was: Wind up the show in the nicest way possible. There was a lack of dignity."

Lorne's words were to ring in Michael's ears for the rest of his television career. When "Little House" and then "Highway to Heaven" were going to end, Michael always made sure his cast and crew knew about it in advance. It's not that Michael had become clairvoyant, it's that *he* decided when the series would halt production, *not* the network.

"When 'Bonanza' dropped out of the top five ratings after so many years, they were in the middle of a week of shooting," Melissa Anderson, Landon's young costar on "Little House," would explain years later, "when suddenly they were canceled. That hurt Michael and I know he'd never want to be canceled. He'll quit while we're riding high."

By the time "Bonanza" was canceled, Michael was more than ready to exit the show. He'd been earning ten thousand dollars a week for his role of "Little Joe" for several years, and he and Lynn and the children were living in splendor on a lush Beverly Hills estate. Money was no longer a priority.

A self-confessed workaholic, Michael didn't miss a step in his path toward building a career for himself as a writer and director. In less than a year, he wrote and directed the NBC pilot *Love Came Laughing,* which launched the short-lived network series, "Love Story," and he directed Paul Winfield in *It's Good to Be Alive,* a TV autobiography of baseballer Roy Campanella's battle against paralysis after a near-fatal automobile accident.

Then fate crossed Michael's path with that of Ed Friendly, a TV producer searching for a network and the financing for a series pilot based on the homespun books of Laura Ingalls Wilder. Considering Michael's obsession with family, and his connection with NBC, the melding of Landon and Friendly appeared to be a perfect union. And it was . . . for a short while. In the final stages of the short-lived relationship, however, it was anything but friendly.

Eight

If Ed Friendly's young daughter hadn't been sick and stayed home from school, chances are "Little House on the Prairie" would not have become a television series. But she *was* sick and she *did* stay home and she spent most of that time rereading all nine of Laura Ingalls Wilder's vivid tales about pioneer life in the mid-1800s. Curious as to why the classic children's books were holding her attention for hours upon end, Friendly picked up one of the books and began to read. Like his daughter he found it impossible to put the book down. At that point, Friendly knew he had the makings of a TV series, possibly even a hit TV series.

It took Friendly eleven months of negotiations with Harper & Row, Ingalls's publishers, and with a lawyer for the Ingalls estate, but finally he got the rights to the books which, by then, had been popular for more than forty years. Friendly then spent another year of his life developing a two-hour script for a "Movie of the Week" pilot. It was at that point Ed Friendly brought the project to Michael's attention, and he, in turn, brought it to the attention of NBC.

"You have to go somewhere to get your financing," Friendly later explained. At the time, Friendly thought it was a right and bright move. In hindsight, he realized it was a big mistake.

With Michael starring as Charles Ingalls, the upstanding head of the Ingalls household, the two-hour NBC pilot of "Little House on the Prairie" was telecast on March 30, 1973, and garnered the highest ratings of any made-for-TV movie aired that entire year. It also earned the distinction of being the highest-rated "NBC Movie of the Week" in the history of the network. Armed with those statistics then, it wasn't surprising that the NBC brass decided to immediately exercise their option to produce an hour-long series based on the Ingalls books.

Since Michael was under contract to the network to develop future series, a deal he had made when "Bonanza" was canceled, there was no problem in setting him up to star in the series. But Landon's contract also called for him to be executive producer. And therein rested a problem. Since it was his project and he owned the rights to the books, Friendly should have been the executive producer. Friendly wasn't happy about this billing, which then made him coexecutive producer with Landon, but he nevertheless agreed to the shared billing. That was Friendly's second, biggest, and final mistake in the launching of "Little House."

As Friendly would later explain: " 'The Movie of the Week' pilot had been pretty close to the script we had developed. But when it came to the series, Landon started to exert his own philosophy and judgment. And NBC was caught in the middle."

Friendly wanted the series to remain true to the books. "I wanted it to be authentic, to follow the major ingredients of the seventeen-year saga. I wanted to illustrate the growth and development of the characters as they matured." Michael wanted changes made. For instance, in the book, a plague of grasshoppers descends upon the Ingalls farm, threatening to destroy their crops. Landon told Friendly that would be too difficult to direct. Instead he wanted to make it a hailstorm.

"I'll never forget being in a meeting one day, discussing a certain scene," Friendly continued, "and Landon said: 'I think I should react. I should jump on my horse and follow them.' At this point I said: 'The only problem with that is that you don't *have* a horse!' "

According to Friendly, Landon also was unhappy about the series showing his children going to school barefooted. "He didn't understand why his kids on the show had to be the poorest kids in town. What could I say? That was the point of the Ingalls books.

"Another time, during a meeting to discuss the family's first home, Landon decided he couldn't direct the episode if he lived in a sod house. A network programming executive backed up Landon, saying he, too, would find it 'depressing to live in a sod house.' I said, "How would you know? Have you ever lived in one?' "

It was at that point, Friendly recalled, that he asked himself what he was doing there. They were changing the series to be the antithesis of the Ingalls books. It was as though the Ingalls family was living in a mansion and had everything but a Cadillac. "At that point I renamed the series, 'How Affluent Is My Prairie.' " Friendly laughed, but not without a trace of disgust in his voice.

Landon wanted everything neat and tidy, with beautiful characters on the show. That meant new stories that had absolutely no bearing on the Ingalls books would have to be written. "No problem," Landon said. "I'll write them." Since Michael had a contract with NBC, the network gave him carte blanche to create a "Little House on the Prairie" with whatever materials he wanted, be it sod, clay, or logs. The writing was clearly on the wall. Friendly was dismayed and thoroughly disgusted.

"I concluded the people I was dealing with just didn't have the talent for adaptation," Friendly said, adding, "In our industry, they can always get rid of a producer or a writer, but they never know how to deal with a performer.

"When NBC absolutely refused to stay within what I considered to be the normal boundaries of reasonable adaptation, I said I wouldn't have my name on the show. The way Landon wanted to do it, I was convinced it would just be a carbon copy of 'The Waltons' on CBS."

At that point, Ed Friendly became the second name on a growing list of Michael Landon detractors. David Dortort, the creator and executive producer of "Bonanza," had preceded him. Friendly and Landon parted company on anything but friendly terms, and a short while later, his title of coexecutive producer was removed from the credits and the tag line "An NBC production in association with Ed Friendly" was added.

"It sounds as though it was a power struggle, but it wasn't," Landon would later say. "I was way too powerful for Ed to make it a power struggle. That would have been like an ant attacking an elephant.

"No, the whole conflict with Ed," Landon explained, "was over the fact that only one person can operate a show. I don't work by committee. The things we fought over were not very important, but they were very important to him. He wanted me to glue on a beard. He wanted the children to be in their bare feet. I mean, I am not going to have kids in bare feet working in the Simi Valley with thorns, pieces of glass, and rattlesnakes. It doesn't make the show better or worse if they're wearing shoes. It just keeps the kids from bleeding to death or getting pneumonia."

"Truthfully," Landon later confided, "I wasn't in love with the pilot script, but I liked the people. The people were so good I knew the show just had to work."

Although he tempered his remarks, Friendly was bitter about the experience. "It is as ludicrous for Landon to be executive producer as for me to walk in and ask to be the star of a series," Friendly told an interviewer not long after his departure. "I don't have anything for or against Michael Landon. I think he's an adequate actor. But that doesn't make him a good actor. He's quite a good director, but he's a mediocre writer; he's not a producer, and he's not up to the task of adaptation. Other than that, I think he's perfect."

So although Friendly was the man initially responsible for bringing "Little House" to the attention of NBC, and retains the rights to all nine of the Laura Ingalls Wilder books upon which the show is based, he has never taken any pride in the series. Nor has he received any significant credit for having been involved with the show. The same certainly is not true for Landon, who took great pride, as well as all of the credit, for the show's success. And deservedly so.

"Little House on the Prairie" made its debut on NBC in September 1974, with Landon portraying Charlie Ingalls, the kindly father of the pioneer family, and Karen Grassle as his equally kind and understanding wife, Caroline. Melissa Gilbert portrayed their oldest daughter, Laura, and Melissa Sue Anderson played their youngest daughter, Mary.

The show was as much of an instant hit as you can find in the pages of TV history books. It hit the Nielsen Top 10 with its premiere episode and remained there for almost the entire eight years it was on the air, dumbfounding the programming cynics who had insisted that sex and violence were the key ingredients of any successful television drama. The cynics, along with Ed Friendly, had been wrong. The network and everyone around him may have doubted the show's ability to hold an audience, but Michael had followed his instincts. And he had been right. The American public had a hankering for the good old days when life was simpler, a family was not a broken home, and a friend was a friend.

"Many people don't know what goes on inside of families, other than their own," Michael explained shortly after the series debuted. "They only know another family from TV. And what you get in most TV families is an idiotic father and inane discussions, nobody saying anything to anybody. Our show gives people hope. Kids, especially, take heart. If their family life isn't so hot, we give them hope that when they grow up and have their own families, they'll be all right, and won't make the same mistakes."

If there had been any doubt in Hollywood minds as to whether or not Michael Landon had longevity in the business, "Little House" had certainly erased it. By the time Michael decided to draw the series to a close after its 1981–82 season, he had become one of the most powerful forces at work in television, especially at NBC television. He also had become a multimillionaire, earning around eight million dollars a year from his combined efforts as executive producer, chief writer, part-time director, and full-time actor.

Despite the money and power, however, Michael retained his self-deprecating sense of humor. In his office at Paramount there hung a cartoon showing two people dining at a posh restaurant and discussing a gentleman passing their table. The caption read: "Oh, he's one of those hyphenates. Writer-producer-actor-asshole!"

Nine

"Little House" was shot on location in Simi Valley, California. Dry, arid, and often 110 degrees in the shade, this locale is just over the horizon from the populous San Fernando Valley, both of which have served as locations for westerns since the earliest days of West Coast movie-making. It was in Simi Valley that NBC constructed the entire make-believe town of Walnut Grove, Minnesota, as well as two rivers and the Ingalls farm. The interior scenes were filmed at Paramount, the studio where his father had been denied entrance and where Michael had found himself starring in "Bonanza" only a few years later. The location filming in Simi Valley was done in the winter months, when the weather was at its coolest, with the interior scenes shot on the show's permanent sets indoors on Paramount's vast soundstages.

Since it was more than a hour's drive from his Beverly Hills mansion to Simi Valley, Landon would arise at five in the morning and an hour later, after working out in his gym, he'd be wheeling his classic 1967 Aston Martin DB6 north, down the San Diego freeway. He claimed not to mind the drive because it gave him time to think, to organize his thoughts for the day's shooting. However, the truth was that Landon rarely slept more than four or five hours a night and would be up at 5 A.M., whether he was working or not.

"I couldn't sleep eight hours a night. I mean, after four hours you can forget it," he once confided to a reporter. "The eyeballs are just open. There's no way I could sleep. I absolutely don't know how in the hell people do it. I get up every morning, no matter where I am, between five and five-thirty and I'm wide awake. And I always see "Johnny Carson," so it always turns out to be about four hours of sleep."

But even if he hadn't been an early riser, Michael still would have been one of the first people on the set. It was one of the few places where he felt alive. The set was his world, where he was at his best, where he was happiest. Lynn had the house, the car, the household staff. Michael had the set, a world of his making, the safe harbor he had yearned for as a child. On the set, he was loved, nurtured, and respected. He was safe, and most importantly, he was in control.

"The thing that appeals to me about doing a television series is the continuation of associations with people, everybody involved in the making of the show," he once explained. "It's nice to come to work and have friends and people you know, instead of bouncing from one place to another and meeting people for two weeks, four weeks, or six weeks and then moving on, which is how it is if you're making movies."

So Michael stuck to television, carefully handpicking his crews and using them on each of his series and his infrequent TV movies. More than ninety percent of his one hundred and twenty-five crew members on "Little House" had worked with him on "Bonanza." They knew him, knew how he worked. They were comfortable with him, and they trusted him. More importantly, he trusted them.

"We're all like a regular family," Melissa Gilbert was fond of saying. "We sit down for meals together and behave as if we're all related. We tell each other jokes or chat about each other's families. The only word to describe Michael," she added, "is super. He's very honest and always true to himself. When my own father died, he took me off in a corner and had a long talk with me until I stopped crying. Now he's another father to me—the greatest person in the world."

And, indeed, "Little House" did seem more like a family outing than the stressful big business atmosphere of producing a weekly hourlong television show on time and within budget. And that is something for which Landon should take credit. He was, for the most part, a benevolent boss who occasionally would halt production for an hour or two of impromptu baseball or horseshoes.

"Nobody worked *for* Mike, they worked *with* him," explained Bill Kiley, retired NBC publicist who worked with Landon on both "Bonanza" and "Little House."

"The guys would kill for him," echoed Victor French, a longtime Landon crony who appeared in "Little House" as Charles Ingalls's scruffy neighbor, Isaiah Edwards. "Mike sets the tone. He's straight with them and they respect him. I've known him for eighteen years and we've never had an argument. He doesn't walk around with this massive ego, but he does speak his mind. Act like a jerk and he'll tell you you're a jerk."

Not long after that French *did* have a temporary falling-out with Landon when he left "Little House" to star as Chief Roy Mobey, a white police chief coping with a black deputy trained in big-city criminology, in his own television series, "Carter Country," an ABC sitcom. Victor had felt that NBC was underpaying him. So when he received an offer to star in his own series, he jumped at it. Apparently, he didn't realize that Landon would take his departure as a personal rejection, although it's difficult to believe French didn't know his mentor better than that. At any rate, relations between the two chilled, to put it mildly.

"Michael felt he'd lost a brother, a member of his very tight group on the show," recalled Kent McCray, Landon's longtime friend and business partner, explained. "Michael always looked to Victor to play important scenes. He turned to Victor to hash out problems in a script or on the set. Then Victor was gone and it hurt."

When French learned that Michael was upset about his departure, he set up a meeting with Landon and the two men settled their differences.

"I understood why Michael was upset," French said. "It was like I had deserted him. But after I heard there was a problem, I went to talk to him directly and explain everything. It was all settled and forgotten in five minutes."

After "Carter Country" died a forgettable death in its second season, French wound up back on "Little House," and he and Landon continued their friendship, both on and off the set, until French's death from lung cancer in 1989.

In return for their loyalty, and their labors, Landon's casts and crews have been generously rewarded over the years. One Christmas, for example, he gave everyone on the show an expensive stereo system. Another year he handed out $1,000 gold watches. Yet another Christmas everyone working on "Little House" received an $800 gold coin in a case with the inscription: "To My Solid Gold Crew."

It wasn't only at Christmas that Landon was generous, either. On many occasions he would hand out gifts—for a wedding, a birthday, an anniversary—or spontaneously reach into his pocket for cash. On one afternoon, when a writer happened to be on the set, Landon walked up to an unsuspecting crew member and slapped a stack of bills in his hand, congratulating him on the birth of his second child.

"We want you to know this is the last envelope you're getting from us," he said with a grin. "So you better stop humping!"

Another time, only weeks before announcing he had decided the 1981-82 season would be the finale for "Little House," Michael handed out more than $125,000 in Christmas gifts to his 130 cast and crew members, giving them each a $500 video disc player. He then did the same for the 100 people employed on the other series he was then producing, "Father Murphy." Then, at the show's annual Christmas party, Landon announced he was planning to use the same crew on future projects after "Little House" ended in March.

In an unstable business, where people earn high salaries but often endure months of unemployment between jobs, Michael Landon was a bastion of security. But there were other reasons for the loyalty he enjoyed.

"He doesn't scream," a crew member explained. "This is a tough town and there are a lot of directors and producers who abuse people by screaming at them. Mike doesn't do that. Also, everything on 'Little House' runs like clockwork. Mike has a partner, Kent McCray, who has been with him for years, and Kent makes it all run smoothly. If we're supposed to shoot a scene at noon on Monday, we shoot it at noon Monday. People get to leave early and go home to their families every night."

Add to this the fact that Landon worked faster than anyone else in Hollywood, that he was always under budget and split the surplus dollars among his crew, and you have a multitude of reasons as to why his crew members through the years have sworn the Michael Landon total pledge of allegiance.

Love. Truth. Decency. Those were the staples that "Little House" wholesomely peddled to the American public. Those were the commodities that Michael Landon sold to *himself.* No matter that they were sometimes too unrealistic, too idealistic. No matter that he sometimes failed to live up to his own standards in real life. Michael was totally committed to his virtuous vision of the American family, a vision created by someone who had spent his formative childhood years wishfully looking from the outside in at other families. It was a dream and yet it was a very successful dream.

"I think the show is successful because it's what real families are all about," Michael said four years after the series had been on the air. "Despite what you see in the movies and on many TV screens, loving families do exist. They don't spend hours screaming and yelling at each other. What's wrong with a show that depicts family love? I feel sorry for people who think 'Little House' is too sweet to be true. That's baloney."

"I hug my kids every day," he continued. "I tell them that I love them and they tell me they love me, too. My wife is the most important person in the world. My kids say 'Yes, sir' when I give them an order and they don't scream or make demands. In other words, most families are based on love and attention—not on screaming, yelling, and the lack of expressed affection."

As "Little House" continued its residency in the Nielsen Top Ten, Michael gradually replaced Robert Young as America's father figure, issuing forth his ideas about the relationship between children and parents. Overcoming silent anger was a major theme on the show, and one of Michael's favorite topics.

"I'm trying to show people that if you talk things out, you can make it and do well together and be happy," he explained, adding, "I think I have a bead on what the American people want in their lives. Everybody has lost their kids, lost their families, lost control . . . 'Little House' shows another side."

If that sounded familiar, it should. It's Michael Landon's childhood revisited, rewritten, and repackaged. Virtually everything he wrote was a reflection or a reinvention of his childhood. The 1976 NBC made-for-TV movie, *The Loneliest Runner,* for example, was about the humiliation a young boy suffers from being a bed wetter. *Sam's Son,* a 1983 NBC movie, was the tale of a young boy, a loser, who learns to throw a javelin farther than anyone else and becomes a winner.

"What I find is that the scripts I write usually come out happy and family-love oriented. That probably stems from the disharmony I experienced in my unhappy family as a child," Michael acknowledged in a moment of insight. "I put a pencil to the paper, but it's something inside of me, or outside, that actually creates the situation, the scenes, the words. I really don't know what happens.

"I sit down with the Ingalls family characters in mind and it begins to flow, and what goes on those pages is like a miracle. While I'm writing I lose all sense of myself, where I am and what I'm doing. i don't even know what time of day it is. I write a whole show straight through in one sitting. Then when I read it, what's on those pages is incredible to me. The content of each script always has something to do with faith and God, subjects that have never been big in my conversations. It's as though God is the one writing those scripts, using my mind and my hands.

"Maybe," he concluded, "I am a religious man and don't even know it."

Maybe. But as generous as Michael Landon was, he also had a dark side and could be cold, arrogant, and cutting, especially if he felt his authority was in any way threatened.

"Mike is very difficult to get to know," admitted Katherine MacGregor, who appeared as Mrs. Oleson on "Little House" for all of its eight seasons. "He keeps people at arm's length. Maybe it's insecurity. I've very rarely seen him lose his temper, but once in a while when it comes out, it's frightening. In fact, I have spent a lot of time hating Mike, and then a lot of time praying for him."

"You never win an argument with Michael," confessed one of his series stars. "He uses sarcasm. He punishes you in sly, nasty ways. If one of his actors gives him any trouble, he tries to destroy their scenes. If it's time for a shot, he'll stick out his tongue and try to make them laugh or forget their lines. Or when it comes time for somebody else's close-up, he'll announce that there isn't time for that shot. Or he'll go ahead with the shot, but cut them out of it later in the editing room. He uses all his skills as weapons for control."

Sarcasm. It was a weapon which, along with his humor, Landon honed to a fine art years ago in Collingswood. It was his first choice weapon of defense, and it could be deadly.

From the beginning, when he was just starting out on "Bonanza," Landon showed a certain disregard for the social conventions usually associated with doing business in Hollywood. Instead of engaging in the pleasantries and pretenses beneath which the stars and the star makers interact, Landon seemed to take great pride in showing his disdain for the rules of the game. Indeed, if a writer was offended during a Landon interview, because the star had either refused to answer a question or had mocked him, Landon didn't care. He actually seemed to delight in rebuffing reporters, as though it were some perverse badge of courage.

"I want to feel like I can say anything to anybody and that I don't need to owe a favor to anyone," was his explanation to an inquisitive reporter, who had been privy to a press conference during which Landon had managed to alienate most of the writers in the room. It wasn't a new experience for Landon who, during the height of "Bonanza," was making an estimated ten thousand dollars a week and had been asked by a newspaper reporter if he felt embarrassed about "being overpaid."

"Let me ask you something," Landon had retorted. "How much do you make a week?"

"Three hundred and fifty dollars," the reporter had replied.

"Well," Landon said with a smile and a shrug, "I guess we're both in the same boat."

Ten

While Charles Ingalls was toughing it out on the family farm in Simi Valley, poor but proud, the man who breathed life into him every week was comfortably ensconced in a magnificent walled and gated eight-acre Beverly Hills estate. Situated just around the corner from Pickfair, the famous home of Mary Pickford and Douglas Fairbanks, the Landons' rambling 35-room New Orleans-style colonial home was surrounded by manicured gardens, courtyards, a larger-than-usual swimming pool, a tennis court, and a pool house decorated exactly like the Ponderosa ranch house from "Bonanza."

Like the walls protecting it from passersby, the home was brick. "I grew up in a brick house and I've always liked them," Landon once explained to a visitor, adding, "Of course, you could have put that whole house in the living room of this house."

The interior of the seven-bedroom Beverly Hills house was as elegant as the exterior. The drawing room walls were made of wood panels imported from Europe. The chandeliers were from the finest crystal. An intricate tea set sat on a coffee table and the marble fireplace was fashioned in England.

In the immense downstairs family room, with its wall rack filled with wine bottles, were souvenirs from Michael's "Bonanza" days — Pa Cartwright's desk lamp and a hat rack from a "Bonanza" saloon. The interior of the pool house, which doubled as a projection room where Landon would often screen Disney films for his children, was also a replica of the Ponderosa ranch house, decorated with "Bonanza" maps and other paraphernalia from the Cartwright home.

It's no small wonder that Landon once told an interviewer, "It's great to be home every night, sleeping in my own bed, even in these meager surroundings. I love my own place, and with a series you have that."

In the middle of all this luxury sat Michael Landon. With his penchant for casual clothes — tight blue jeans, cowboy boots, and open-collared shirts which unfailingly exposed a gorgeously tanned chest highlighted by an expensive gold chain, Michael didn't look as though he belonged there. So it isn't surprising he once confided to a close friend that he had never really felt at home in all that splendor.

"Lynn," he had explained, "is a very aristocratic kind of woman. She likes all of this. Me, on the other hand, I'm basically a blue-collar kind of guy. I like living at the beach. I like being in my shorts. I like eating dinner without any clothes on, which is why I don't like having maids and nannies, household staff, in the house. Besides," he had laughed, "you can't have a decent argument with them around. It would all end up in the tabloids after they're gone."

So Michael bought a beach house, a five-bedroom oceanfront property, and the family divided their time between Malibu and Beverly Hills. And at least once a year the entire Landon brood plus friends would go to Hawaii, one of Michael's favorite vacation spots. They would usually stay at the swank Kahala Hilton on Diamond Head. But even while on vacation Michael could not stop working. One year he wrote five hours worth of screenplays during what was supposed to be his vacation.

"Hawaii is fine for a couple of days, and it's nice getting away," he would admit, "but before long I'm with the pad and pencil writing 'Little House' scripts. My wife, Lynn, loves Hawaii, too, but I can't get up every morning and lie in a chair and watch my skin roll up. I've got to write. So I write.

"Some people see my working too hard as a negative thing," he continued. "It's even bothered Lynn at times. But I told her that overworking is my life, and if I wasn't deeply into my work, I'd be real difficult to live with."

In the last year of "Little House," Landon doubled his income, along with his work load, as the creator, producer, and sometimes writer of "Father Murphy." A frontier drama, "Father Murphy" starred Merlin Olson as a good-hearted drifter who ends up running an orphanage and, for the good of all concerned, posing as a priest.

Although the series was set in the Dakota territories, circa 1870, much of the show was actually filmed on location in Arizona. This left Michael dividing his time between Los Angeles and Phoenix. Not unlike the old days on "Bonanza," when Michael would jump on a plane as soon as filming had wrapped up, he found himself constantly on a plane to or from Arizona. It was a grueling schedule, but he loved the pace, the action, the challenge.

"I don't know how he does it," Olson told a friend. "It would kill anybody else. I know he's driven, we're all driven. We all have our devils. I don't know what Mike's are, but I know they must be powerful, just by the pace he sets for himself."

"Once you've gotten something off the ground, it's tough to keep the enthusiasm going," Michael once confided. "The stories are different, but the sets are the same, the people are the same. There are certain limitations because the same people are back every week. That's why I like busting off and doing different things, the TV movies, for instance. I like the change and the challenge."

"Father Murphy" went on the air November 3, 1981, to lukewarm reviews. And although the show never amassed the viewship of Michael's other series, it stayed on the air through June 17, 1984. By that time, of course, Michael was already heavily involved with "Highway to Heaven," the only series he owned in entirety.

Merlin Olson had first met Michael in 1977, shortly after signing an NBC network contract. Only a month or two later, he was contacted by Landon, who wanted to know if Olson would be interested in portraying John Garvey, a new character he was adding to "Little House." It was the beginning of a lengthy partnership between the two men. Olson appeared on "Little House" for three years.

"I've never met anyone in this business as versatile as Michael," Olson recalled not long ago. "I saw him do things that anyone else would have thought were impossible, like sitting down in the rain rewriting a script right there on the spot so that we could keep on shooting. He had a respect for family and a respect for decency which transcended the dollar.

"And," Olson continued, "he had a wicked sense of humor. I remember a particular scene we were shooting on 'Little House' which involved a crow having to land on my head.

"Well, the crow kept flying up into a nearby tree," Olson said laughing, "and Michael kept having to go up after it. Finally, after this had

Michael Landon, America's latest heartthrob, circa 1956.

Michael's first big break in the movie business came when he was cast in the low-budget 1957 horror film, "I Was a Teenage Werewolf." Here he's seen in full werewolf regalia with his leading lady, Dawn Richard.

Michael and Dodie Fraser, his first wife, caught in a casual shot at a Hollywood premiere. Despite outward appearances, there had been trouble in the marriage almost from the start in 1956.

Michael and Dodie allow photographers into their Hollywood home for some informal magazine shots of their life together not long after he got the role as Little Joe on "Bonanza." They divorced after six years together in 1962. Michael later confided he had married her because he couldn't bear to hurt her son Mark, above, whom he later adopted. (Larry Barbier/Globe Photos, Inc.)

An animal lover, Dodie at one point had collected a menagerie of ten pets, including a boa constrictor and two dogs. Michael wasn't overjoyed at living in a zoo but he nevertheless posed with four of the seven family felines in this 1960 publicity photo. (Larry Barbier /Globe Photos, Inc.)

Michael, posing with co-stars (left to right) Pernell Roberts, Lorne Greene and Dan Blocker, gained the reputation of being an arrogant hell-raiser because of his temper tantrums on the "Bonanza" set. The real problem, however, was his heavy drinking and reliance on prescription drugs.

Lorne Greene, seen here with Michael on the set of "Bonanza," not only played his father on television; he also played it in real life. Lorne was one of the few people in Tinsel Town that Michael came to trust and respect. Greene's death from cancer in 1987 affected him more than his own father's.

Michael posed with his "Bonanza" co-stars Dan Blocker, Lorne Greene and David Canary, who joined the series to fill the gap left by the departure of Pernell Roberts in 1966. Standing next to Landon is David Dortort, creator and producer of the long-running western, who was not a Landon fan, despite their fourteen-year working relationship.

Michael married former model, Lynn Noe, his second wife, the year he divorced Dodie. The marriage appeared to be a happy and lasting one. It was a shock to Hollywood and to Landon fans when Michael filed for divorce April 16, 1981, after almost 20 years of marriage, citing "irreconcilable differences."

Michael and Lynn at home in Beverly Hills with three of their four children. Clockwise Michael, Michael Jr., Lynn, holding Shawna, and Leslie. (Herb Lewis/ Globe Photos, Inc.)

Michael and Lynn were among guests attending a party hosted by Kirk and Anne Douglas after the Palm Springs premiere of the 1967 Columbia Pictures film, "The Happening." Michael had been dating Lynn for months before he finally summoned the courage to ask his first wife, Dodie, for a divorce.

Michael Landon, in his Charles Ingalls western garb, posed for this NBC publicity shot on the specially-constructed Simi Valley set of "The Little House on the Prairie." Landon came into his own with the family show, becoming producer, writer, director and star.

Here is Michael in a happy moment with his TV "family" on the set of "Little House." <u>Clockwise</u>: Melissa Sue Anderson (Mary Ingalls), Melissa Gilbert (Laura), Michael, Karen Grassle (Caroline), Lindsay Greenbush (Carrie) and of course, Bandit, their faithful dog.

Michael always loved animals. Here he's seen relaxing on the set of "Little House" with Bandit.

Ed Friendly brought "Little House" to the attention of NBC and developed the series pilot. Although his name remained in the credits as executive producer, Friendly and Landon had a bitter falling out over Landon's need to have everything his way.

Michael was a mentor to Melissa Sue Anderson, who played his daughter on "Little House" and, like Michael, was interested in becoming a director. As a result, she was always at his shoulder when he was directing a segment of the series. Whatever difficulties he had in dealing with adults, Michael had a remarkable rapport with children.

In 1976, Ernest Borgnine guest starred as an angel Jonathan in "Little House." Ten years later, Michael himself played Jonathan Smith, an angel in his hit series "Highway to Heaven."

Michael took his humiliating childhood experiences and wove them into the mega hit NBC-TV movie about a young athlete, "The Loneliest Runner." Naturally, Michael wrote, directed and starred in the 1976 film.

Michael joined the ranks of Hollywood's most beloved and enduring stars when he received his own star on Tinsel Town's Walk of Fame on August 15, 1984.

Victor French, who died in 1989, was like a brother to Michael. The two met on "Bonanza" and continued working together on "Little House" and "Highway to Heaven."

Michael and Victor French with the closeknit crew on location for "Highway to Heaven."

The filming of his 1983 TV movie, "Love is Forever," nearly ended in disaster when Michael's relationship with the director, Hall Bartlett, turned sour. Despite this informal beach shot, his lovely co-star, Priscilla Presley, was even reduced to tears by his aloof treatment of her on the set.

Dean Martin took to the podium and put Michael in the hot seat for a 1984 "Dean Martin Celebrity Roast," which was taped at the MGM Grand Hotel in Las Vegas.

Soon after the son of his best friend and manager, John Warren, was born with Down's Syndrome, Michael became active in fundraising for the Down's Syndrome Parents of Los Angeles group. Each year he hosts Michael Landon's Celebrity Gala and appears in as many benefits as possible, like this one in Filmland, CA. (Ralph Dominguez/Globe Photos, Inc.)

Michael and his new bride, the former Cindy Clerico, posed for these pictures only minutes after their Valentine's Day wedding at his Malibu beach-front home in 1983. Cindy was two months pregnant at the time.

Michael and third wife, Cindy, with their children, Jennifer and Sean. (Bob V. Noble/Globe Photos, Inc.)

The Landon family posed for this group shot shortly after Michael married third wife, Cindy. (Left to right) Josh and Mark, Michael's adopted sons from his first marriage; Leslie, his oldest daughter from his second marriage; Cindy and Michael; Michael, Jr., Christopher and Shawna, Leslie's two brothers and sister. (Ralph Dominguez/Globe Photos, Inc.)

Michael appeared with his good friend and fellow tennis player, Johnny Carson, on "The Tonight Show," only a month after having been diagnosed with inoperable pancreatic cancer on April 9, 1991. It was his last public appearance. He died on July 1, 1991.

happened three or four times, he decided to get the crow's attention by putting pieces of rotten meat on the top of my head. It worked. The crow flew right to its mark, picked up the piece of meat, and flew off, but not before it deposited a mound of you-know-what at almost the exact spot where the meat had been. Well, Michael thought that was one of the funniest things he'd ever seen. He just loved that and laughed about it for a couple of days. He had a wonderful sense of humor and a great laugh. I have wonderful memories of that laugh and just sitting on the set, listening to him tell stories. I think one of the things that made Michael so special was his personal involvement with everyone around him, his willingness to share of himself."

Despite the high brick wall surrounding the mansion, Michael and his family were not immune to crises. The first major problem to strike the household was when Lynn's daughter, Cheryl, was almost killed in a late-night automobile accident in 1973 while she was a student majoring in drama at the University of Arizona.

As Michael would later recall, "She was coming home from a fraternity-sorority gathering with four friends in a tiny little Volkswagen, and they were struck by a Ford going more than eighty miles an hour. There were four people in the car and she was the only one who survived the accident. But it was real touch and go for a while and she almost died, too. It was a terrible, terrible accident. She was in the hospital for months."

As a result of the heavy doses of painkillers Cheryl was given during her lengthy recuperation, she became dependent on drugs and spent two years, from 1975 until 1977, in a California clinic trying to overcome her habit. "She was so heavy into pills, anything she could get her hands on, that she overdosed several times," Michael confessed. "You tell yourself 'I can handle this. I can take care of it. I'll just give her a lot of love.' But the fact is that simply doesn't cut it. What you're giving them, in many cases, is exactly what they don't need. What they need is someone to say 'Knock off all the crap and take care of your own life. You're responsible for it. Nobody can save you except you.

"The problem is, when kids are on drugs, they'll lie to you," he continued, recalling the family's heartbreaking experiences with their twenty-four-year-old daughter. "They'll promise you anything. They are always going to stop, but nobody gets off of drugs because somebody else wants them off. They get off because they realize that they are alive, that they're worth something as people, that they're better than that."

Driven to the breaking point by Cheryl's addiction, they finally convinced her to accompany them to CEDU, a California drug rehab center which Michael described as "a wonderful place."

"I'd tried everything else in California, but there's this rule, it's a state ruling, I guess, where rehab centers don't receive funding unless they have a staff psychiatrist. Unfortunately, the majority of psychiatrists prescribe drugs to drug addicts, which never made sense to me. The shrink would tell us: 'Don't worry that I'm giving her some drugs. I'm only doing that because it helps her speak honestly to me and gradually the drugs won't mean anything.' 'Well, then don't give her any,' I'd say. And I'd get into an argument because that was the way it worked.

"The night I left her at CEDU was a very emotional experience for everyone involved," Michael continued. "Cheryl was honest enough to say she was scared of being left because she didn't have any drugs. But from that time on our house was a much more relaxed household because I knew that when the phone rang at three in the morning, it wasn't going to be a hospital calling to tell me my daughter had overdosed.

"It was a tremendous weight off my chest, feeling that I had picked the best spot for her at that time. I helped her navigate her way by taking her there. There was no fence. She could have left at any time. But," he concluded, "I made it clear that I was in touch with the police and that if she came home I would have her arrested."

Cheryl later married James Wilson, a manufacturer's rep, and made Michael a grandfather for the first time in 1986.

No sooner had the family survived Cheryl's drug crisis, however, than they discovered their daughter, Leslie, who was a twenty-two-year-old college student at the time, was suffering from bulimia.

"It really started out as a lark," Leslie would

later recall, "with a whole bunch of girls pigging out, as they will, when they first get into a sorority and it's the first time you can keep your room filthy and eat any of the junk you want without hiding wrappers under the bed."

What may have begun as a lark, however, ended with Leslie spending several years in group therapy before conquering the emotional disease. Like her older sister, Cheryl, however, Leslie did overcome her problem and in 1982, pursuing her childhood dream of being an actress, she joined the cast of "Little House" in the recurring role of Etta Plum, Walnut Grove's pretty young teacher. By the time Leslie, then twenty years old, joined the show, she had already appeared on "Little House" four times in small parts, beginning with her debut at age twelve in which she played a child dying of plague.

"I have mixed emotions," Lynn confided about Leslie's lifelong ambition to be an actress. "I know this is what Leslie has always wanted, ever since she was a little girl doing skits at school. But I wasn't happy that she quit USC to work on Michael's show. I would have preferred she finish her education. Right now she's working on her father's show, but when that ends she'll be competing with thousands of other young girls. She's very competitive, but she has also led a very sheltered life."

Michael disagreed. "You can't guard your children against disappointment," he said. "If you're not ready to be disappointed, then you should find some other way to make a living because that's what acting can be: A series of disappointments. On the other hand, it can be a tremendously rewarding career. Leslie's like me," he concluded. "She's tough and she's competitive. She's also a poor loser. She'll do just fine."

Despite Michael's obsession with work, and their problem with the children, the Landons' marriage seemed rock solid, especially in Tinsel Town where couples seem to change partners so frequently it's almost as though they were involved in some perverse emotional square dance. They were not part of the glitzy Hollywood crowd, preferring instead the company of mostly non-industry people, married couples with children, like car dealer Howard Barish and his wife; Kent McCray, Michael's closest friend as well as his producer, and his family; and John Warren, another trusted friend and advisor, and his family.

"I don't know another big star really well, except Lorne Green," Landon once confided. "I don't know any executive at any studio, except the guys I work with at NBC and I bet we don't talk more than once or twice a year. I'm your typical old-time work guy, and I like it that way. I don't owe anybody anything." Landon's only real Hollywood friend was Johnny Carson, a Malibu neighbor with whom he often played tennis and infrequently dined. Like Landon, Carson, too, was a loner. Well-known by the public, respected and feared by the entertainment industry, Carson was not really a member of any particular Hollywood circle.

"With a wife and seven kids, there was always a problem," Michael would later concede. "Lynn and I fought a lot about jealousy, about my being too tied up in my work, about this and about that. But," he had added, "I figure if you don't have these kinds of problems, life would just come up with some other unpleasantries for you. Nobody's perfect. Not Charles Ingalls. Not Michael Landon."

So it was a great shock to Hollywood, as well as the rest of the world, when Michael moved out of the couple's Beverly Hills home in July, 1980, and took up residence at their Malibu beach home. He released a simple statement: "I have moved out. Lynn and the kids are going to take a vacation in Spain. When they get back, I will spend weekends with them. This is our way of trying to work out our problems. I hope nobody makes a big deal out of it. We are not talking about divorce."

But it was a big deal. Michael knew it, and Lynn knew it. Suspecting that Michael was involved with another woman, Lynn had hired a private detective to find out whether her suspicions were true or false. She was devastated when the detective turned in his report. Her suspicions were true. Michael was involved with another woman, pretty twenty-one-year-old Cindy Clerico, whom he'd met on the set of "Little House," where she was working as a makeup artist and sometime stand-in.

"I remember the first time I saw her," Michael would recall years later in a *Life* magazine interview shortly before his death. "It was on 'Little House' and we needed a stand-in for the children. Cindy was hired because she was blond and short, only five feet two. Her first assignment was to sit on a stump while I focused a lens on her. And I thought, 'What a fascinating young woman.' She had the most wonderful smile. Then I saw the way she was with the kids on the show, so open, natural, and warm. And she had a great laugh.

"There was something about her that was fascinating. I found myself watching her through stronger and stronger lenses. I was like a kid with a crush, and I felt very guilty about those feelings because I was married to Lynn and I had five children. So even though after seventeen years my wife and I had grown apart, I was devoted to the children. I tried to squelch my feelings for Cindy, but they only got stronger. I just fell more and more in love with her the more we were together, and I made sure we were together every chance we could.

"One evening, after a party on the set, I asked if I could see her that night. She said yes and we agreed to meet at her apartment. But when I arrived and knocked on the door, nobody was home. I decided she must have had second thoughts. So I got in my car, but just as I started to drive away I heard honking, and there she was. She'd stopped at a gas station on the way home."

After that, Landon admitted, he couldn't keep away from her. "At lunchtime I would meet her on one of the Walnut Grove sets so we could hold hands and kiss. The more I saw her, the more I loved her, the more I wanted to be around her, no matter how painful it would be for Lynn and the children."

The irony of Michael's infidelity could not possibly have escaped Lynn, the woman he'd met eighteen years before under almost the exact circumstances on the set of "Bonanza."

Eleven

The year 1981 was undoubtedly the worst year Michael had endured since departing Collingswood more than thirty years before. He was beleaguered by the press, especially the tabloids, who were giving him almost weekly beratings in front page headlines about his separation from Lynn; and he was constantly being hounded by the paparazzi trying to catch a photograph of him and his new love, Cindy.

Professionally, his relationship with Cindy was proving ruinous. Not only was he being lambasted by the press, there were people at NBC who were questioning his ability to continue to portray Charles Ingalls, happily married frontiersman and devoted father. Michael suffered an even greater blow when Kodak announced it was removing him as its television spokesman since his image as a father at home no longer was positive and truthful.

"The relationship lasted nineteen years," Michael would explain when interviewers inquired how a thrice-married man could portray such a saintly father on television. "I don't consider that a failed marriage. I don't think it was a disaster. We produced some terrific kids. We just didn't grow in the same direction. We became different people. We both changed.

"To stay with someone when you no longer have anything in common is the cruelest thing to do to a child. It's much better to divorce and have two parents who are happy. I don't know if Charles Ingalls would have stayed married to Caroline as long as he did, except that it was a long way to the next house in those days."

Then on March 15, 1981, his mother died. Michael and his seventy-one-year-old mother had been estranged for years, even though they were living in the same city only miles apart. He felt no obligation to either his mother or his sister, Evelyn, both of whom had become increasingly eccentric as the years had rolled by.

Peggy O'Neill and Evelyn, who had adopted the name Victoria King during a brief fling as an actress in the fifties, were sharing a small apartment in a run-down Los Angeles neighborhood, along with Evelyn's teenaged daughter, when they were robbed in August, 1981. They naturally filed a police report, which then reached the ears of the tabloid press, one of which then ran a story about their financial difficulties. MICHAEL LANDON COLD-SHOULDERS HIS AILING MOTHER AND SISTER, screamed the headline for a story quoting Michael's mother as saying: "I don't know where he lives. I never bother him because he doesn't like me asking questions. He's quite secretive. He keeps me at a distance. I don't even have his phone number. Why should I? I'm not very important. I'm just his mother." Evelyn was quoted as having angrily said, "I never mention his name."

Naturally the tabloid press didn't examine the reasons for Michael's behavior, they simply took the words of his mother and sister and printed them in a damning article. The truth was that Michael had been financially assisting his mother and sister for years. When Peggy had broken her hip in late 1980, he had paid for her hospitalization and, despite his own misgivings, had even gone to visit her at the hospital. He had also unbegrudgingly paid Evelyn's medical bills in June, 1981, when she suffered burns in an accident at home. But that was where his involvement with them ended. He was not going to spend time with them or incorporate them into his life. Why should he? As far back as he could remember his mother had caused him nothing but grief and aggravation. He had drawn a line through her name after his first marriage to Dodie, and he'd never erased it.

"When I was a kid, I loved her," he confided to a friend. "But when I grew up it was a different feeling. I felt sorry for her and I had to divorce myself from loving her because, otherwise, all that pain would have been transferred to me."

It was true that his mother didn't have his telephone number. It was true that as soon as either his mother or sister managed to somehow wrangle his number out of a friend, he would have it changed. He didn't want them calling him, haranguing him. He didn't want them to know where he lived for fear they would show up, uninvited, and cause a scene.

It had taken him years to overcome the guilt he felt about about having disavowed his mother and his sister. Now he wanted absolutely nothing to do with either of them.

"I was afraid of her, and my oldest kids were terrified of her, because you never knew who she was going to be," Michael recalled several years after his mother's death. "She spoke with a lot of different accents, and she'd use them all in one conversation. The irony of all this was that my mother apparently was a wonderful person to people who didn't know her. I don't know how many times people have come up to me and said, 'Your mother was the sweetest!'

"I don't know," he had sighed, "maybe she was to them. When they tell me that, though, all I can think of is the time she came after me with a knife and there I was in my jockey shorts, jumping fences in front of the neighbors, trying to escape."

Although, by his own design, they had been virtual strangers for years, the death of his mother filled Michael with a strange mixture of sadness and relief. It was the end of a chapter in his life, the end of the family, be it as it was. Despite everything that had transpired in the past, Michael felt a sense of loss. He realized that Peggy's death had left questions in his mind that would never be answered.

Less than two weeks after his mother's death, Michael was forced to deal with his sister, who suffered a nervous breakdown and had to be institutionalized. Michael had her transported to a private hospital and paid her expenses. Although the press attributed Evelyn's mental state to the death of her mother, chances are that the real cause behind her collapse was due to having *lived* with Peggy all those years.

Then almost a month from the date of his mother's death, Michael made a decision regarding his future. Citing "irreconcilable differences," he filed for divorce from Lynn on April 16, 1981. Everyone, except Michael's closest friends, was caught totally off guard because Michael and Lynn had been talking about a reconciliation. At least that's what Lynn had *thought* they were talking about. Thus, of all the people who were shocked by Michael's divorce petition, it was Lynn who was the most stunned. She had learned of it while on an Easter vacation in Acapulco with the children. Her brother, Bob, had telephoned her with the news that Michael had filed the divorce papers. She flew back to Los Angeles in a daze.

"I loved him and I just couldn't shut the door

on all the years we shared," she would later confide to friends. "I honestly hoped that it was some form of temporary middle-aged love affair. I believed that if I were patient, he would come to his senses and return to the family that loves and needs him."

Unlike Dodie twenty years before, Lynn was not amiable to the divorce. She was angry and she was bitter. She had been a devoted wife and mother to seven children, and she had been betrayed, callously cast aside for a younger woman. "I was too busy being the kind of wife Michael wanted me to be," Lynn later confided. "As a result I lost myself little by little. I made Michael my god."

"Lynn," said a close friend, "will never forgive him for ruining everything she held precious. She's a very sad and disillusioned lady."

Under California's community property laws, Michael would have to split the fortune he had amassed during his marriage to Lynn. And it was quite a fortune, estimated at approximately forty million dollars.

Since he was then making an estimated eight million dollars a year from the series alone, the settlement promised to be one of the most costly divorces in the history of Hollywood, topped only by that of Michael's good friend and tennis-playing pal, Johnny Carson. But no one, not even Michael, expected Lynn to go after him with such a vengeance.

The first thing Lynn did was to invite the *National Enquirer* into the home for an "Exclusive" interview less than a month after Michael had filed for divorce.

"I still can't believe that we have become just another American divorce statistic," she told the reporter. "We had everything. The Landon family was close, happy, and secure. We had it all, or so I thought. Our marriage was built on a foundation of trust. Or so I thought.

"I know that Hollywood is littered with wrecked marriages," she continued, "but I sincerely believed ours was different. Now it's another statistic. Life goes on, and the children and I will, too. I loved him very much. I've lost a lot. The children have lost out on having a father in the house. And I think Michael has lost a lot, too."

If Michael felt a loss, however, he was feeling it from a distance. While Lynn poured out her anguish and hurt to the nation's number one tabloid newspaper, Michael and Cindy were happily vacationing in London. Michael had become as inseparable from Cindy as he had twenty years before from Lynn.

Shocked that Lynn would actually discuss their marital situation in a tabloid interview for all the world to read, Michael did several interviews himself after returning from England.

"My marriage to Lynn wasn't dynamic toward the end, but there were an awful lot of good years. That's why it was so sad for me to see a lot of her anger come out when I left her," he told an interviewer. "But if two people aren't each giving one hundred percent to the marriage, I really think in the long run it's better for both parties if they divorce. There's nothing worse than people who obviously should not be together who spend their entire lives torturing each other. They only get angrier and angrier doing something they feel they shouldn't be doing. That was one reason," he confided, "I'd go around screaming at people—at home and at the studio, at everybody in sight—banging down telephones, swearing and yelling. I simply wasn't happy. I wasn't where I wanted to be, with whom I wanted to be.

"I begged my own parents to stay together when they had difficulties," he recalled, "and they let me talk them into it. Looking back, I don't think it was a favor to them or to myself. Who needs a kid to make decisions? When two people are miserable together and can't make things better, one or both should decide to end the marriage."

"Michael has made his choice," Lynn countered. "And I think at this point it would be best for me and the children if he made his affair legal and married his girlfriend."

Although Lynn and Michael were divorced in December, 1981, they were still battling over the community property settlement a year later. According to Lynn, Michael was earning $665,000 a month and she needed $75,000 a month to maintain herself, her home, and her children in the manner to which Michael had helped them grow accustomed.

The list of estimated monthly expenses filed

by Lynn Landon's attorney at the Beverly Hills courthouse in early 1982 was subsequently published by *STAR* magazine, and offered an eye-opening glimpse into Hollywood life styles of the rich and famous:

Household Expenses	Est. Monthly Expenses
Domestic help	$2,967.00
Food and beverage	3,257.00
Gardening	1,520.00
Household	1,733.00
Linens	363.00
Insurance	1,592.00
Security services	3,820.00
Repairs and maintenance	1,962.00
Utilities	1,000.00
Telephone	500.00
Laundry and dry cleaning	600.00
Miscellaneous	395.00
Payroll taxes (domestics)	216.00
Mortgage	1,322.00
Property taxes	813.00
Home improvements & furnishings	4,000.00
Auto expenses	600.00
Secretarial and bookkeeping	1,500.00
Total	**$28,160.00**

Lynn Landon's Personal Expenses

Auto expenses	$1,600.00
Medical expenses	2,840.00
Clothing	5,600.00
Entertainment	2,500.00
Gifts	1,800.00
Travel	6,431.00
Contributions	1,000.00
Personal care	359.00
Miscellaneous	638.00
Preparation of Tax Returns	350.00
Total	**$23,118.00**

Children's Personal Expenses

Clothing	$3,000.00
Governess	1,344.00
Lessons, camps, etc.	1,300.00
Parties and toys	498.00
Allowances	672.00
Gifts, audio/video equipment,etc.	1,385.00
Travel	3,735.00
Education	2,310.00
Cheryl Pontrelli	2,000.00
Medical expenses	1,250.00
Auto expenses	2,800.00
Miscellaneous	2,797.00
Leslie's personal care	100.00
Total	**$23,191.00**

Total Monthly Expenses	**$74,469.00**

Michael might tout himself as a blue-collar kind of guy, but in truth, he earned more in one week than his blue-collar counterpart would earn in ten years.

After having spent the first three months of 1982 embroiled in arguing about the settlement, the only thing Michael and Lynn had agreed upon was the undisclosed amount of Lynn's temporary support. Throughout the entire divorce proceedings Michael had been totally uncooperative, leading Lynn to become even more determined and angry. At one point she switched attorneys and then had Michael's business manager subpoenaed to uncover what Michael really *was* worth.

They were running out of time to settle their differences, a situation which would lead them into the Beverly Hills courtroom on April 27, when Michael finally relented and Lynn received an estimated settlement of $26 million, which included the $3.5-million-dollar home the couple had shared. Michael had wanted to sell the estate and then split the proceeds with Lynn; but she wanted to continue living there because it was the family home, her children's home, and she intended to have it stay that way.

In the meantime, Michael, according to a friend, reportedly looked like a man carrying all the weight of the world on his shoulders. Usually an upbeat guy, Michael had become sullen and withdrawn. He seemed to be in a world of his own, an unpleasant world according to the gloomy expression he frequently wore at that time. Although he attended the 1981-82 season's wrap-up party for "Little House," he was anything but the life of it, and, unlike the Michael Landon of old, left early without even saying goodbye.

He was an unhappy man with a multitude of problems. Yes, his divorce from Lynn had been final and he'd bitten the bullet about the settlement. He'd made his peace with his mother's death. He'd even taken care of his sister, Evelyn, and her costly institutionalization. He didn't even mind that Kodak had dropped him as their spokesman. What he hadn't managed to come to grips with was the alienation his divorce from Lynn had created with his children.

"I think one of the toughest things for kids to accept during a divorce," Michael conceded, "is that there is somebody else in the world who's alive besides themselves, and that this person has to live and has to try and be happy, and has to work at it."

By the time the divorce had become final, Michael and Cindy had already started living together at his Malibu beach house, which he had improved by adding a $29,000 bathroom with a gigantic picture window overlooking the Pacific Ocean, and a new pool with a jacuzzi designed by Maj Hagman, a neighbor and the wife of another TV superstar, Larry Hagman.

But it was a difficult time. Cindy would stay at Michael's beach house during the week, then spend the weekends at her apartment in town while Michael saw his children who remained loyal to their mother, Lynn. It was an uncomfortable situation for everyone, but there didn't seem to be any other choice.

"The children had a problem with it," he explained several years later, "but the older kids, who weren't living at home, were totally accepting of the divorce. It was Leslie and Michael, Jr., who had the toughest time accepting it. I had told them over and over that it was best for me and their mother, but they didn't buy it. They were very angry because they felt I wasn't being a perfect father. They wanted me to stay married, whether or not I was happy.

"They pretended to accept Cindy, but they weren't being honest with their feelings. It was very uncomfortable. I finally told them, 'Okay, be the way you are. Feel what you feel. You want to be angry at me? Fine. I can handle that. But I can't handle it when you emotionally lie to me.' I also told them I didn't want to see them, and I didn't want them to see me, until they were ready to see me."

Michael's world seemed to be falling to pieces, with large chunks of it constantly landing on his head. Nothing was going right. Not only was his relationship with his youngest children intolerable, the resultant stress was creating problems for him and Cindy, and they were having frequent fights. Equally distressing was his relationship with NBC. It had suffered immeasurable damage when the network Michael had so profitably served for more than twenty-two years insisted he continue producing "Little

House" another two seasons, something he was loathe to do.

Michael had argued with the network brass, pointing out all of the rational, well-taken reasons he was against the continuation of the series. However, when the network had threatened to keep "Father Murphy" in its doomed Sunday night time slot against "Sixty Minutes," the popular CBS TV news magazine, Michael had caved in to their wishes. He agreed to continue to produce, direct, and write "Little House" through the 1983-84 season. But he had told the NBC programming executives he was *not* going to appear on "Little House" on a regular basis. He also negotiated a further extension of his network contract, allowing him to continue to develop and produce both TV movies and, after the end of "Little House," yet another hourlong series, which he would own outright.

Since he'd already announced to his cast and crew that "Little House" would end at the conclusion of the 1981-82 season, Michael was then faced with the task of having to renegotiate contracts. The crew, of course, was no problem. They were all ready and waiting to return to work. It was the "Little House" stars that represented a difficult situation, since several of them, including Melissa Gilbert and Karen Grassle, were not interested in continuing their roles on the series. They felt, as did Michael, that eight years was enough. Like him, they wanted to move on, to expand.

Faced with this dilemma, Michael did a fast

shuffle. He wrote Melissa Gilbert out of the show, and out of the schoolhouse, by having her get pregnant. Then he replaced her with another teacher, Etta Plum, portrayed by his twenty-year-old daughter, Leslie. He altered the focus of the series, from the Ingalls to the Carter family, introducing the characters of John Carter, played by Stan Ivar, and his two sons. He then negotiated with the other members of the original cast to either remain with the series or to agree to make infrequent appearances on the show. It was a clever ploy. And it worked. The public continued to watch "Little House" for two more seasons, although without Michael's regular appearances as Charles Ingalls, the ratings did begin to slip. "Father Murphy" also remained on the air until June, 1984.

In 1982, however, Michael made a move that turned out not to be either clever or smart. For reasons understood only by himself, he chose to accept the starring role in a film to be directed and produced by someone other than himself. The results were disastrous—for everyone concerned.

Twelve

Perhaps Michael needed a rest. Perhaps he simply wanted to get away from his problems. Or maybe he just fell in love with the script. Whatever the reasons behind his acceptance of the starring role in the 1982 film *Love Is Forever,* it didn't take long for Michael, or anyone else involved with the project, to realize it had been a mistake of major proportion.

The film, which was to be shot on location in Thailand, was based on the true story of John Everingham, an Australian journalist who had been forced to leave Keo, his Laotian fiancée, behind after being expelled from Laos as a spy in 1978. Everingham had subsequently trained to swim underwater using scuba gear in the treacherous Mekong River running through Thailand. In one of the decade's more adventurous feats, Everingham had rescued Keo by swimming to freedom along the river bottom, with her in tow, while the Pathet Lao forces fired at them from above.

The film, which starred Michael as the daring Everingham, featured an international cast including Edward Woodward, Jurgen Porchnow, Moira Chen, and Priscilla Presley. It was being produced and directed by Hall Bartlett, who had read a news story about Everingham and had spent four years putting the film together after buying the rights to the story. Bartlett's original plan was to produce a film for theatrical release. But he was unable to get the financing and distribution until 1981, when 20th Century-Fox agreed to underwrite the project.

Bartlett had been in the process of casting the film when his two daughters, both dedicated viewers of "Little House on the Prairie," suggested that Michael Landon might be perfect to portray John Everingham. Bartlett sent the script to Michael, who read it and eagerly accepted the role. Landon even got NBC interested in putting up part of the film's financing. Thus, what had originally been a movie for theatrical release became an American television movie to be aired on NBC, with 20th Century-Fox exhibiting the film, theatrically, everywhere else in the world.

Bartlett was so ecstatic over this turn of financial events, he didn't bother to question or balk when the contract's fine print read that Landon also would receive billing as the film's producer. Bartlett wasn't even concerned when Landon didn't show up in Bangkok for the weeks of preproduction rehearsals he'd planned.

"He said, 'I don't like to leave my game in the locker room,' " Bartlett would later explain, "So, knowing how quickly he could learn his lines after all the television he'd done, I said okay."

A couple of days prior to the start of principal photography Michael arrived in Bangkok, accompanied by Cindy and his son, Michael, Jr. He was, he said, ready to begin work. Everything appeared to be moving along well, an illusion that was quickly shattered within the first three days of shooting. Landon, the cast and crew quickly realized, was going to be a problem because he could not adjust to having someone else dictate to him. He had to be in charge. He could not operate within the normal parameters of simply being an actor. By the end of the first week, he had managed to alienate everyone around him, including Andrew Laszlo, the film's highly acclaimed director of photography, who had filmed the NBC miniseries "Shogun" and at that point had thirty full-length feature film credits listed below his name.

"He told me that on 'Little House' his camera crew could do a hundred setups in a day. When I reminded him that this was not episodic television, but a large-scale movie, he became angry," Laszlo recalled.

Landon went to Bartlett and complained about the amount of time Laszlo was taking to set up his camera shots. "He demanded that I fire Laszlo," Bartlett said, "and when I refused, he sulked."

The following week, when the company was filming near the Burmese border, Landon took it upon himself to begin directing the film while Bartlett and Laszlo were busy elsewhere with the actors. "I looked up and there was Landon setting up the camera and arranging extras," recalled Bill Thomas, the film's costume designer, "as though he were the director, not Bartlett."

A few days after that, when Bartlett and Laszlo again were not on the set, Landon took the camera and half the crew and left to film a scene under his direction. At that point, Bartlett was forced to make an agonizing decision: He could either attempt to control Landon nicely, or he could fire him on the spot. If he chose to fire him the film would be delayed—all of the scenes with Michael would have to be reshot with a replacement—and that would put the film off budget and off schedule. Bartlett swallowed his pride, but he did turn out a memo to cast and crew, pointing out that he was the only director on the film.

According to Bartlett, Landon never again tried to direct the film. Instead, he became nasty, rude, and foul-mouthed.

"He constantly mocked me with gestures while I was setting up shots, and he constantly ridiculed Laszlo, verbally, until Andy started vomiting blood and quit the film. It took every persuasive argument I could think of to get him to return. It was a nightmare," Bartlett concluded.

After that, Michael went out of control. He reverted to childish behavior, deliberately distracting the cast and crew with nonstop dirty jokes when he was off camera. Whether he was simply insensitive to the actors trying to deliver their lines, or so caught up in his own ego, is a matter of conjecture. The fact is that by the time the filming in Thailand ended, everyone agreed that Michael Landon in no way resembled Charles Ingalls. Everyone also agreed that Landon had been especially nasty to Priscilla Presley, who unfortunately had accepted her role of Landon's girlfriend as her first major acting outing.

Landon was constantly making fun of Priscilla fixing her hair by shouting over and over again, "It's Charlie's Angels time."

Calling the entire shoot "an emotionally wrenching" experience, Priscilla later acknowledged in a *TV Guide* interview that "I did fiddle with my hair a lot. But so would any woman with long hair in ninety-five percent humidity. But the worst was that he refused to rehearse with me or help me in any way in our scenes together."

What Priscilla didn't tell the interviewer was that, at one point, when the scene called for her to adjust Landon's diving equipment, he swore at her and yelled, "Get your hands off me." When she pointed out it was in the script, he swore again and said, "I don't care what's in the script. How would you like me to start adjusting your bathing suit straps?" Later, in a scene in which he was supposed to dance with her, he refused, embarrassing everyone within earshot.

Bartlett later confirmed Michael's treatment of Priscilla. "He was very cruel to her," he said.

But it wasn't just Priscilla who was the object of Michael's scorn. When Moira Chen, who played his Laotian girlfriend, was preparing for a scene, Landon followed her around cracking dirty jokes, mouthing obscenities, trying to distract her for reasons known only to him. Finally, Bartlett told Michael to leave her alone. And he did, for a while.

Bill Kushner, first assistant director on the film, was amazed by Landon's conduct. "He would storm off the set shouting and swearing that he was leaving the movie, and we should do what he wanted because some of the money for the film had been put up by NBC . . . and that he *was* NBC," Kushner revealed after the film had finally wrapped up and Landon had returned to his "Little House."

"Other times," Kushner continued, "he would give anybody who approached him 'the finger.' He was a horrible person. He couldn't even stand to be upstaged by his son, Michael. He embarrassed everyone, and I'm sure his son, too, by pushing Michael aside after he'd been trying to teach some Thai children English, and began teaching the kids vulgar words."

The night before the company was to leave Thailand, Michael took to the dais to make a short farewell speech at a party attended by Thai government officials. What he said was: "The only time I'll come back to Thailand is if my doctors tell me I only have a month to live. Then I'll return here because time passes more slowly in Thailand than in any other place in the world."

It was no doubt Michael's sense of humor, sarcastic and rude. But nobody laughed. By that time, no one had retained their sense of humor where Michael Landon was concerned.

"The trouble was," Kushner confessed later, "that nobody could do much about his behavior in Thailand because we knew that if he walked off the set the whole project would go down the drain and a lot of money wasted. Now that we're here, wrapping the film in Nassau, the truth can be told. And the truth is that my instructions while we're here is to make sure Landon behaves himself. If he doesn't he will be taken to the airport and put on a plane headed toward Los Angeles."

"It's a pity that this battle developed between Michael and the rest of the crew," Edward Woodward, CBS's "Equalizer," said. "He is a very able, talented actor, but he just could not handle the fact that he had to take orders from the director."

Having brought his film in five days early and on budget, Hall Bartlett carefully tempered his remarks upon his return to the United States. "Michael Landon," he said, "is not the Michael Landon I originally met and came to respect in Los Angeles. I was one of Michael's biggest fans before Thailand, and I really believe if it hadn't been for his power complex, we could have become very close. But Michael can only work in situations where he has complete control."

Michael's response to the accusations and criticism was exactly what one would expect. "I was a coexecutive producer on the film. I had control." Terming the entire filmmaking experience "pathetic," Landon said: "It was a situation where the producer and director drove off and never told anyone from transportation or anyone else where they went. I was a coexecutive producer on that film and I had an entire company of people sitting there and no one could find Bartlett. It's my prerogative as the executive producer to continue. I had the control. I mean as far as I knew, those two guys had been killed in a traffic accident. So I said a prayer for them, and we continued to shoot that afternoon.

"I know Priscilla had a few numbers to say about my conduct," he added, "but I think Priscilla was as anxious to get space as anybody else. She was just starting out. I was never rude to her. It's just that I know a hell of a lot more about the business than Priscilla Presley. I knew I'd been conned the first day of the picture. I'm sure Priscilla didn't know she'd been conned until she saw the film. It's no fun going to the premiere and wanting to throw up."

Don Parker was the representative of the Hollywood-based firm of Percenterprises Completion Guarantor, the insurance company which guarantees a film will come in on time and on budget. If there is anyone who is objective about the atmosphere on the set it is the completion bond representative, who only goes on a film location when there is trouble on the set. In this case, the job fell to Parker, a former TV production manager.

According to Parker, "My only objective is to see that a picture is completed according to the approved script and contract. In this case, I observed all of Mr. Landon's antics and constantly ruled against him and in favor of Hall Bartlett. Landon sincerely believed he had the same power over a director as he does on his

TV series. He was wrong. Contractually, Hall Bartlett was the director and producer. Landon was given the title of executive producer in the credits, but *contractually* he was merely an actor.

"With all the problems—and there were problems—I'm amazed that Bartlett managed to bring the film in on budget and on schedule," Barker had concluded.

Back in Los Angeles, however, Bartlett's problems were not yet over. Michael made one last attempt to gain final control of the film. Going to both NBC and 20th Century-Fox, he made a bid to have Bartlett allow him to edit the film. He was turned down and that was the last Hall Bartlett ever heard from Michael Landon.

When the control was taken out of Michael's hands, he reverted to a child having a temper tantrum, acting out his rage with wanton disregard for anyone else's feelings. This was true in his personal life, and it was true in his professional life.

"The only time I ever saw him get mad," confided Bill Kiley, Landon's NBC publicist on "Bonanza" and "Little House," "was at someone who tried to flex muscle, like the time a director yelled at a standby, or an assistant director yelled at the kids to be quiet off the set. Mike wouldn't put up with it and, truthfully, I've always thought it was because of what had happened to his father."

Perhaps. Whatever the answer, the truth is that the only time Landon lost his cool was when he'd lost control of a situation, whether it was a marriage, a film, or merely an argument. He was, by his own admission, a poor loser.

"Michael's whole thing has always been about control, not money," confirmed Jay Bernstein's on-again, off-again publicist. "He has always been more interested in control over everything than in being a star. In fact, the only problem I have ever known him to have had in his career, has been when someone else has either been in control . . . or when someone else wanted to be in control."

Even Landon, himself, once admitted that "The only bad experiences I've had are the times when I have not had control."

No wonder 1981 and most of 1982 were disastrous years for him. He'd lost control of almost everything. He hadn't been able to manipulate or force Lynn into bowing to any of his wishes. He hadn't won the battle with NBC over "Little House." He hadn't been able to charm his teenaged children back into the fold; and he hadn't been able to sustain his Mr.-Nice-Guy image in Thailand.

Originally titled *Comeback,* and released in Canada with that time, *Love Is Forever* was telecast on NBC in 1983 and received little notice. It will be remembered only because of

Michael's petulant antics on the set and the resultant bad press he received.

Bad press, however, never bothered Michael. He was immune to it. After all, this is the man who, in the midst of an argument with Ed Friendly over the direction "Little House" should take, once retorted: "Yes, I am perfect! It's a problem I've had all of my life!"

Thirteen

Returning to Los Angeles, Michael and Cindy continued living together through the week and spending their weekends separately, while Michael tried to work out the problems with his children. Gradually, he managed to pull everyone and everything together, but it hadn't been easy. It had taken a lot of energy, a lot of time. And Cindy was growing impatient.

After all, she and Michael had been dating since 1980, and living together since 1981. But Michael would not marry her until he had made amends with all of his children. The turning point apparently arrived when Leslie, his oldest daughter from his marriage with Lynn, finally accepted Cindy as a member of the Landon household.

A short while later, during Christmas 1982, Michael asked Cindy to marry him, and to underscore his love and devotion, he gave her a very large, very expensive emerald and diamond ring. It was, he told her, a combination Christmas and engagement present. Michael was always very generous to his family. Cindy was no exception. Prior to their marriage, he had given her a new Mercedes, a diamond watch, and thousands of dollars worth of other jewelry, as well as a membership to an expensive and elite Malibu exercise club. It was also rumored that Michael financed a new look for his bride-to-be by having her jaw broken and reset, and her teeth redone, eliminating a pronounced overbite and exposed gums when she smiled.

Having held off the marriage for two years because he was afraid his children would not accept Cindy, Michael moved swiftly once Leslie had joined the other Landon offspring in their chorus of approval. Besides, Cindy had discovered she was pregnant. So less than two months after the announcement of their engagement, the couple were wed in a small, private ceremony at their Malibu beach house, which only days earlier had been badly damaged by a heavy rainstorm and high waves.

The marriage, on Valentine's Day 1983, was attended by all of the Landon children. After drinking champagne and cutting the cake, the couple left for a week-long honeymoon at the secluded, posh resort, La Samanna Hotel, on the island of St. Martin in the French West Indies.

A week later Cindy and Michael were back in Malibu, making plans for the delivery of their first child . . . and Michael's eighth. She was twenty-six years old and Michael was forty-seven, more than twenty years her senior, with two adopted sons older than Cindy. However, according to friends, it was difficult to tell who was more excited about the forthcoming birth of their child, Cindy or Michael. As though he were directing a show, Michael took care of everything. He reserved two rooms at Cedars-Sinai Hospital in West Hollywood; one for Cindy, himself, and the baby, the other for his young son, Christopher, and his daughter, Shawna, by his ex-wife Lynn. In preparation for the birth, Michael had also regularly attended group childbirth classes so that he could assist in the delivery.

Six months after their marriage, the Landons became the proud parents of a daughter, whom they named Jennifer Rachel. "It was a beautiful and emotional moment of my life," Michael told reporters as the couple left the hospital three days later with their new daughter. "You can't believe what a miracle birth is until you share it." A year later, Michael became a grandfather for the first time when his daughter Cheryl and her husband presented him with a grandson, James Michael Wilson. Three years after the birth of their daughter, Michael and Cindy would have their last child, a son, Sean Matthew.

Since both "Little House" and "Father Murphy" had ended production for their final season on NBC, Michael turned his energies into creating and developing other television productions. He produced and directed "Sam's Son," an autobiographical film detailing his days as a javelin thrower, and he wrote two two-hour movie scripts for "Little House on the Prairie," which he also would direct and produce. In addition, he was busily working on a story outline for a four-hour NBC drama based on the exploits of a World War II hero who led five hundred paratroopers into the Philippines to rescue more than two thousand civilians from the invading Japanese.

Michael's life had at last returned to what he considered normal. He was still working hard, but work was the foundation of his life. "I do work long days," he admitted, "but I've always had to work very hard in order to be happy. I'm not good sitting around. I need to be doing something." Unlike in the past, however, Michael was working for the sheer joy of it, not because he needed an escape from an unhappy marriage or the boredom of a complacent marriage. With Cindy, he was equally alive and happy. So there were lots of good times carved out of his work schedule, sometimes with the entire family, sometimes just with Cindy and his younger children.

What Michael liked best were the times when, dressed in jeans, the whole family would spontaneously jump in the car, go to the movies, and eat out. It was the kind of casual California living Michael enjoyed. He also was pleased that Cindy's relationship with Leslie, who was only six years younger than her stepmother, had become that of sisters. Cindy would help Leslie choose her makeup, style her hair, and pick out clothes.

"The kids think the world of Cindy and I do, too," Michael happily told a friend not long after his third marriage. "She's a great cook, a wonderful mother to them, and a good person to talk to and fun to be with."

He was also pleased that, after several years, Lynn had begun making strides to pull her life together. She had become a businesswoman and had opened a successful Los Angeles boutique, Trios. More importantly to Michael, she had mellowed in her feelings toward him, at least outwardly, thus relieving Michael of the tremendous guilt he had carried with him after the divorce. After all, she was the mother of

149

four of his children and his wife of almost two decades.

"I think Lynn is a much happier person now than she was when we were married," Michael told friends. "She's a much more energetic person and I can see the change in her. She's her own person. She ahs her own business, something I wish she would have done years ago, but she never did.

"I think the divorce really brought her out, made her a more rounded person than she was before. At least, I would like to think so because she's a good person."

And Lynn, although she would never forget Michael's betrayal, finally admitted to a confidante several years after the divorce, "If it hadn't been Cindy, it would've been somebody else. He had reached that point in his life."

Lynn and Michael continued to converse with each other, mainly about the children, but their telephone calls were short and to the point. As Lynn confided to a friend: "We speak without talking. Our conversation consists of 'When will you be by to pick up the kids?'"

Nevertheless, Michael had a sense of well-being, a conviction that everything had turned out exactly as fate had determined his life should be—richly rewarding and filled with love. He was profoundly thankful that the bad times were over. Perhaps that's why, while caught in traffic on the Pacific Coast Highway in Malibu one afternoon in the late spring of 1983, he was reminded of a promise he'd made to God ten years before, when his daughter Cheryl was hovering near death in an Arizona hospital.

"I had made a pact with God," he confided years later. "I'd promised that if Cheryl could be spared, I would do my best to make a product to help people. I'd made that promise at a time when I felt there was very little chance of her surviving. Yet she did survive, against amazing odds. That puts you as close to wanting to keep a promise as anything I can imagine.

"I made that deal with God, I realize now, out of guilt. In my case, the guilt was the feeling that perhaps my life had been too good and that Cheryl's accident was an object lesson. You think a lot of strange things when someone you love, someone so young, may be taken away from you. It makes a lot of changes in you. It makes you realize few of the things you think are important mean a damn thing after all.

"I don't know why it suddenly popped into my mind," he said. "But it did. Everyone was honking their horns and cursing—and I found myself thinking about that promise I'd made so long ago and how it would be good to do a show where people coulds see how much better and healthier it is to go through life being nice."

Michael picked up the children, drove them home, and began thinking about developing a new series, a show that would capture the inherent goodness of mankind. He wanted to create a program that would illustrate how goodness, if given the opportunity, could triumph over adversity and evil.

Although he knew from his past dealings with the network that a concept for an hour program sans violence and sex was going to be a difficult sell, Michael knew the network brass would at least hear him out. Besides, he was convinced that American television viewers wanted to believe, as he did, that there was hope for a better world and that they would set aside time to watch a program that entertained them while at the same time, without preaching, it offered them hope and inspiration.

Being a pragmatist, Michael was also well aware of his successful track record with NBC, which gave him the clout to strongly convince the network that his vision would pay off in high ratings and big advertising dollars. Adding to his strength at NBC was the special relationship he enjoyed with Brandon Tartikoff, who at that point was running NBC network programming.

With all of that in mind, Michael quickly

began working on an outline for his new show. He wrote the pilot script in a week and then set up a meeting to discuss the project with Tartikoff in the fall of 1983.

"He came in, and sat down on the couch in my office," Tartikoff would later recall. He was bronzed and in great shape, and he told me: 'I'm sure a lot of people come into your office and tell you they know how to make people laugh. But I don't know how to do that. I'm the kind of producer who knows how to move people, how to make them feel, how to make them cry. That's what I do.'

"And I said, 'Okay, what's your idea?' Michael said, 'I happen to know that *It's a Wonderful Life* is your favorite movie. I want to do a series with all of those kinds of positive elements in it. I want to play a character who is a positive force, who has the power to change people for the better. I want to play an angel of God.'

"I said, 'You're kidding!'

" 'No,' Michael said, 'I want to portray a character who comes into people's lives and they become better because of it.'

"I told him, 'The press is going to assassinate you. They're going to call you "Jesus of Malibu." '

" 'No,' he laughed. 'I was born Jewish, so it'd be more like "Moses of Malibu!" '

"We discussed the concept some more and I

153

told him, 'Okay, bring me a script.' Four days later he sent the pilot script over."

Despite his belief in Landon's ability to create successful family programs, Tartikoff was more than just a little bit concerned about the concept. He was downright worried. The 1982–83 season had been disastrous. Tartikoff had seen nine of the network's new shows cancelled. Nine new series, nine cancellations. It was not a good track record. What NBC needed was not a low-key series about an angel, it needed a program loaded with action, with adventure, with violence; a series to offset the strength of the ABC hit action-adventure series, "The Fall Guy," starring Lee Majors.

Thus when Michael returned for a meeting with Tartikoff and other NBC executives in the network's boardroom a week or two later, his excitement about the proposed series was in sharp contrast to the mood of everyone else in the room. No one, not even Tartikoff, was verbally endorsing the concept. They had been pinning their hopes on Landon to come up with "a high concept" show, a mix of action, glitz, and hip that would bolster their sagging ratings by attracting the much-desired eighteen to forty-nine age group coveted by advertisers.

"He hit us at a very bad time," Tartikoff would later remark. "We were down and our instincts were at a low point."

Nevertheless, if only to pacify Michael, Tartikoff gave him the go-ahead to shoot the pilot, which Michael did immediately. With the two-hour pilot in hand, Tartikoff screened it for the rest of the NBC brass, and as he later recalled, "It wasn't a screening where people came up to me and enthusiastically proclaimed, 'You did it again, Brandon.'"

Despite the pronounced lack of enthusiasm by his network compatriots, Tartikoff took another step forward with the pilot. He needed a family-oriented program to fill the 8 P.M. Wednesday prime-time spot. So he sent the pilot film to the network's testing facility to be screened for several hundred sample viewers across the country. A week later he had the results. The pilot had gone through the ceiling in terms of viewer response. It had the distinction of being the highest-tested show of any NBC pilot before or since.

If Tartikoff and his NBC executives were stunned, Michael was elated. He'd once again followed his instincts. He'd once again proven himself to be right. He was sitting on top of the TV world, ready to do battle with all challengers from that day forth. Ironically, his first battle was not long in presenting itself when Landon found himself arguing with the network executives over his choice of Victor French to portray his sidekick and helper, Mark Gordon. The network wanted Landon to cast a handsome young guy, who could "bring in the ladies," as his partner-in-charity. But Michael was adamant. He wanted Victor in the role. He would settle for no one else. End of discussion.

And, as usual, he won.

Fourteen

Titled "Highway to Heaven," the series made its debut at 8 P.M. Wednesdays in the fall of 1984, with Michael portraying Jonathan Smith, angel-at-large, and Victor French as the ex-cop and drunkard he had rescued from ruin. To everyone's delight, the series was an instant hit.

Even Ed Friendly begrudgingly admitted the show had its merits. "I was kind of surprised, watching the pilot, to see that it wasn't as bad as I anticipated it being," Friendly told a *TV Guide* writer.

Many of the newspaper critics, however, had a field day with the show. Just as Tartikoff had predicted, they accused Landon of comparing himself to God. They called the series everything from cornball to sickeningly saccharine.

But Michael was undaunted. "What the hell do these press people know anyway?" he asked. "They've never made a picture in their lives."

By the time he had emerged as the star, the producer, and the director of "Highway to Heaven," Michael had earned the reputation of being a contentious perfectionist. He took on network executives, censors, and anybody else who stood in his way or didn't agree with his vision. And proved them wrong.

Adding to his clout with NBC was the fact that Michael owned the "Highway to Heaven" series outright. So when an NBC censor insisted Landon would have to cut a line from an upcoming episode in which a paraplegic, discussing his embarrassment in a bathroom, confides to Jonathan, "I wish I could wipe myself so a nurse wouldn't have to do it," Landon furiously refused and threatened to go to the head of the network, if necessary, to keep the dialogue intact. The censor ultimately reversed his stance, knowing that Landon not only would, but could, carry out his promise to seek out a higher authority. After all, everyone at the network knew that Landon had the ability to work miracles, even at the highest levels of network bureaucracy.

As the producer of "Highway to Heaven," Michael continued his practice, which he had begun on "Little House," of employing a wide variety of physically and emotionally handicapped people. He wrote in characters on

"Little House" who were blind, hearing-impaired, crippled, or who stuttered, thereby guaranteeing employment for handicapped performers who were available but rarely hired by Hollywood filmmakers.

One of the "Highway to Heaven" episodes, for example, dealt with a handicapped attorney courting and marrying a nonhandicapped woman. Since the story line was suggested by James Troesh, a quadriplegic actor married to a woman who was not handicapped, Michael hired Troesh to portray the TV character. He then cast Alan Toy, a paraplegic actor who was a victim of polio, to costar in the episode.

"You can entertain people without abandoning reality," Michael explained. "Stories about individuals coping with their disabilities make the rest of us realize how insignificant our problems really are. These kinds of stories sort of put life into perspective.

"In turn," he added, "handicapped people are pleased to see such stories take their lives out of the closet, allowing the public to see how these challenges have been met and overcome. Most handicapped people want those who are not impaired to look beyond their disabilities and to see the person there."

Not long after the Jim Troesh story was aired on "Highway," Michael learned that a crew member had a son confined to a wheelchair. In despair the young man had quit college and become a recluse for almost two years, not even bothering to open his government disability checks. After seeing the show, however, he told his father he wanted to open a bank account and return to college. Nothing could have pleased Michael more than hearing that story. It was the kind of response he believed he had been put on this earth to elicit. He was convinced it was his destiny to inspire people to rise above intolerable conditions, to achieve their potential and, in doing so, to create a better, more positive world. He had the gift of vision and the ability, as he told Tartikoff, to move people, to make them feel. Television was his twenty-first-century platform of communication, just as books had been to the philosophers and thinkers of the preceding centuries.

No one was more aware than Michael of the odds he had overcome to attain the title of "Mr. NBC," and how fortune had chosen to smile upon him. "I have been incredibly lucky," he confided, "but I've also worked hard, and I've come to realize that you really can't listen to a whole bunch of people because a whole bunch of people are no more right than one person who knows what he wants." And Michael Landon knew what he wanted. He wanted more and he wanted better. He wanted perfection.

With the fervor of a true believer, Michael spent sixteen to eighteen hours a day working on "Highway to Heaven," rereading script, writing scripts, listening to dialogue, trying to capture on film what only a handful of people ever see or comprehend.

"Everything Michael did had a message," Jay Bernstein once said. "He was someone who wanted to save America from itself. He was more a philosopher/writer than a producer of television stories."

Two years after "Highway" had hit the airways, Landon announced he had asked Lorne Greene to appear in a guest-starring role on the series, portraying a down-and-out actor who actually gets a glimpse of God, a glance that changes his life forever.

"Mike and I have wanted to work together ever since 'Bonanza' went off the air," Greene said during a press conference heralding the reunion of the two. "But Mike didn't want to use me on 'Little House' because he said, and I agreed, that it was too much like 'Bonanza.' We thought the audience would probably just sit there in the living rooms saying, 'Why don't Ben and Little Joe let on that they know each other?' "

The show, which marked the first time the two had appeared together in thirteen years, was filmed the week of November 19, 1985, and aired in early 1986. Less than a year later, David Dorfort announced he was at work on a sequel to "Bonanza" titled "Bonanza: The Next Generation," which would be a two-hour movie for TV syndication. Lorne Greene would recreate his original role of Ben Cartwright, but instead of being called "Pa," he would be called "Grandpa" by Dirk Blocker, son of the late Dan Blocker.

Dortort wanted Michael to recreate his role of "Little Joe," and Michael seriously considered it, not because he needed the money or of any loyalty to Dortort, but because of his friendship with Lorne. Only a short while after Dortort announced his plans for the "Bonanza" sequel, however, Lorne Greene was hospitalized, first for a hernia operation and then for cancer. Since it was doubtful that Lorne would be able to do the picture, Michael declined to recreate his role and Dortort subsequently changed the story line. He hired John Ireland to portray Ben Cartwright's brother, and had "Little Joe" lost in the Spanish-American War, never to be heard of again. The sequel was filmed in Tahoe, where the original had been shot. But it came and went, leaving hardly a trace of "Bonanza's" original grandeur in its wake.

Despite the fact that they had not worked together in thirteen years, Lorne and Michael had continued the close relationship they had begun while costarring together on "Bonanza." They still talked on the telephone and they still would have dinner together, although not with great frequency. So Lorne's illness a shock to Michael.

Michael visited Lorne several times during his illness. In fact, he visited the older man only the day before Greene's death on September 11,

1987. According to the nurse on duty at St. John's Hospital in Santa Monica during Michael's last visit, he had walked up to Lorne's bedside, grasped the older man's right hand with both of his, smiled, and said, "How ya doin', Pa?"

Although weakened from the cancer and in obvious pain, Lorne had smiled back and whispered, "Okay."

The two had exchanged few words because it was too difficult for Greene to talk. So Michael stayed fifteen minutes without speaking. He just held Lornes' hand in his. Finally, he got up and slowly walked away. When he reached the doorway he turned and looked for a long time at the man half-asleep in the bed. Then he turned and strode quickly down the corridor. There were tears in his eyes.

Later, after Lorne was gone, Michael would recall his visit. "He looked at me and slowly started to arm wrestle," he said, "just like we used to in the old days on 'Bonanza.' He was Ben Cartwright to the end. He was ready to die with no complaints. I never stopped seeing Lorne as my dad," he added. "Lorne was a solid pillar for both me and Dan Blocker. I'd known him for more than half my life, and he'd been my father for fourteen years on 'Bonanza.' You don't just quit being a son or a father. I'll always consider him my Pa."

With Lorne's death, only Michael and Pernell Roberts were left of the original "Bonanza" cast. Victor Sen Yung, who had played Hop Sing, the Cartwright's humorous and eccentric cook, had committed suicide in 1981.

Perhaps it was the result of Lorne's death, or perhaps it was because of Cindy's insistence, but in 1987 Michael announced he would do three more seasons of "Highway to Heaven," and then he was taking a year off to travel around the world with his family.

In December 1988, the year following Lorne's death, Michael also came close to death when Nathan Trupp, a mental patient wanted in connection with several murders in New Mexico, shot and killed two security guards at Universal studios, before being felled by a barrage of police bullets. He had claimed to be on a "mission from God" and, as he toured the sprawling 420-acre Universal studio lot on his $17.95 general admission ticket, had asked several employees where he could find Michael Landon. Unable to locate Landon, Trupp walked off the tour tram and went to the guardhouse at the entrance to the compound, where he demanded to use a studio phone to speak to Landon. When the guards refused, the forty-two-year-old man walked away, only to return a moment later. He pulled a gun and shot both men through the head, killing one of them instantly. The other died a short while later at the hospital.

While this real-life drama was being played out at Universal, Landon was twenty miles away in Culver City, directing an episode of

"Highway" on the back lot of MGM. None of Landon's television series was ever filmed at Universal. So it will forever remain a mystery as to why the gun-toting Trupp was so convinced that Michael was on the Universal lot.

In May 1989, however, death did strike near Michael once again, when his friend and costar, Victor French, was diagnosed with advanced lung cancer.

French, who had previously portrayed nothing but bad guys because of his large frame and menacing countenance, gave Michael full credit for his successful TV career, claiming Landon was the only one who had recognized he could play a good guy after having spent twenty years portraying killers and rapists. He would often laugh about Michael having rescued him from a life of ongoing crime when he cast him in the role of Mark Gordon on "Highway to Heaven."

Despite a brief falling-out when Victor, feeling that NBC was paying him less than he deserved on "Little House," left the show to star in his own series, "Carter Country," on the ABC network, Michael and Victor were as close as brothers. Victor was one of the few people who could exert any kind of influence over Michael.

When Michael was working day and night on "Little House" and needed a break, for instance, it was Victor who walked into his office, put his hands on the desk, and glowering at Landon said, "Get yourself out from behind that desk. We're going fishing." "And," Michael would later laugh, "we went fishing.

"That's one of the things I always loved about Victor," he had added. "He could always make me see what was really important."

One of the things that was most important to Michael was directing. In fact, he once confided that of his four jobs — acting, directing, writing, and producing — he found directing to be the most difficult, and the most rewarding.

"When I'm directing," he had explained, "everything is a challenge and maybe that's why I like directing best. I know I don't like other people directing my material. I found that out when I did those 'Bonanza' scripts. I'm not saying the shows I wrote weren't directed well. It's just that they were directed differently than I would have directed them."

Nevertheless, in an attempt to slow down and reduce his sixteen-hour-a-day work schedule on "Highway," he chose Victor to divide the directing chores with him. As a result, Victor directed one out of every three episodes of "Highway to Heaven," giving Michael a much-needed break.

When Victor entered Sherman Oaks Community Hospital on June 7, 1989, Michael was devastated.

"He's the best friend a man could have," Michael confessed to colleagues. "My whole family adores him. I can't bear to see him suffer. I can't believe this is happening. We knew there was a terrible fight ahead, and the chances of winning were slim. But we swore to fight to the end. Victor would do everything he could to beat the disease and I would give him every ounce of support humanly possible."

Michael kept his promise. He visited Victor throughout his hospitalization, and even made certain that the June 16, 1989, rerun of "Highway" carried a special message from the cast and crew to his dying friend.

"Dad is going through hell but when Michael comes around, he perks up," Victor's daughter, Tracy, told a friend. "He becomes his old self. It's miraculous. You get the feeling when you see them together that time is standing still, that the pain is going away and Dad is going to beat this. It's a marvelous thing to see such true friendship between two wonderful guys."

But the pain didn't go away and Victor didn't beat the cancer. Along with Victor's children, Victor, Jr., and his twin daughters, Tracy and Kelly, Michael kept an all-night bedside vigil with his friend of thirty years, and was there when Victor died in July, less than a month after having seen Michael's message on the series.

Michael was heartbroken by Victor's death because he and Victor had become as close as brothers and, as Victor had once jokingly pointed out, the two had spent "more time together than a married couple."

According to Victor's wishes, his son organized a party which was guaranteed to make sure there'd be no tears by those attending. A lavish bash, the party was held at the Gene Autry Museum in Griffith Park. It began when a plane flew overhead, trailing an irreverent last message from the departed host. And it ended when the guests could hardly stand up from having ingested as much food and booze as they could hold.

According to actors Ned Beatty, Hal Burton, and Bill Kiley, who were among the invited guests, it was a not-to-be-forgotten farewell. Upon their arrival, guests were given party packs of "Victor props," including whoopy cushions, by waitresses dressed in miniskirted cowgirl outfits. Tex Mex food was served and rock and roll music kept the party swinging. Michael and Cindy, along with the entire cast of "Carter Country," crew members from "Little House" and "Highway to Heaven," were among the guests, as were various guests stars from the series.

Despite the festive air, however, Michael could not pump himself up to be in a partying mood. Victor's death had forced him to begin thinking about his own mortality.

Michael was a bundle of contradictions. He was a physical fitness nut who had a gym that would make any health club look underprivileged installed at every house he ever owned. And he used it regularly. It was a habit he had developed as a teenager. Whenever he was depressed, which had been often in those early days, he'd work out. As soon as he broke into a sweat, he told a friend years later, he'd always feel better. He also was an early-to-bed, early-to-rise kind of guy. But he never missed his friend and neighbor, Johnny Carson, on "The Tonight Show."

Yet, despite his concern for his physical well-being, Michael was a heavy smoker, often smoking as many as four packs of cigarettes a day. "Victor and Michael always had goofy bets going on as to who could quit smoking first," Bill Kiley recalled, "even as far back as the 'Bonanza' days. Victor would inhale so deeply we swore his socks must've been smoking." Like Victor, Michael also was a heavy drinker and loved junk food, especially fried foods, and his eating habits were, to put it bluntly, atrocious. He'd usually skip breakfast and lunch, stoking himself on cigarettes and coffee throughout the day. Then he'd eat two heaping platefuls of food at night, much to the consternation of both Cindy and the Landon family doctor who, at one point, had told Michael he couldn't continue with his haphazard eating habits. But Michael had only laughed and made a joke out of the conversation.

"Why not?" he had asked the physician. "Horses eat that way and they get along just fine!" The fact that he was not a horse did nothing to persuade Michael to change his lifestyle.

Cindy, who was into health foods and, unlike

Michael's other wives, was a nonsmoker, then stepped in and seriously tried to wean him off fried foods and get him to stop smoking. It was a campaign she had been carrying out since before their marriage. And although she had been somewhat successful in the food area, she had failed to deter Michael's smoking. After Victor's death, however, Michael cut down on his smoking and ultimately quit altogether.

Having seen the pain Victor had endured and his struggle for breath from his cancerous lungs, Michael was frightened that he, too, might end up with lung cancer. So, not long after Victor's death, he had made a doctor's appointment, which was not like Michael, and gone in for a chest x-ray which, much to his relief, revealed his lungs were clear, except for the normal congestion found in people who smoke.

Nevertheless, it was at that point, with Cindy's support, that Michael quit smoking. With her encouragement he also cut back on his fried food intake and began eating more vegetables, chicken, and fish.

As Michael had promised Cindy, when "Highway to Heaven" ended in August, 1989, he planned to take a year off to spend with her and their two children. But, somehow, he never got around to it.

Under his contract with NBC, Michael had one more film to produce and then, unless he wanted to continue his relationship with the network and renegotiate his contract, he would become a free agent. After thirty years of serving the NBC network so well, so profitably, the thought was appealing to him.

"I remember the last time I met with Michael," Brandon Tartikoff recently recalled. "It was in June, 1990, at the network's annual affiliate's meeting in Washington, D.C. Michael was one of several major NBC stars to receive a Lifetime Achievement Award for the many years, and the great programming, he had contributed.

"Anyway, we sat and had a drink together before the tribute at the hotel where we were both staying and we discussed our lives, the past, the present, and the future, and the changes that we felt we should each make," Tartikoff continued. "Michael felt it was time, after almost three decades at NBC, to move on."

Michael produced, directed, and starred in his last NBC movie, *Where Pigeons Go to Die,* the story of the relationship between a ten-year-old boy and his grandfather, in the summer of 1990. Costarring Art Carney, Cliff De Young, and Robert Hy Gorman, the two-hour TV movie was telecast January 29, 1991. But by that time Michael had already moved on. He had created, written, directed, and starred in a new pilot for a new series on a new network.

As he told Cindy, he just couldn't stop working. He'd tried to slow down after the end of "Highway," but he had become restless and irritable. Work was his source of self-esteem. Work was his joy. Work was his life, and nothing, not even Cindy and the children, could substitute the adrenaline Michael felt when he was hard at work, creating, writing, and directing. But he would try. For the sake of his family, he would try to slow down, to spend more time with them. After all, he told friends, he *was* over fifty.

Fifteen

Kent McCray, whom Michael had first met when he was the series' assistant director for "Bonanza," was Michael's closest and most trusted associate. With Kent at the helm of any project, Michael could relax. The two were partners, with Kent doing the day-to-day chores involved with production, and Michael doing the creative work. It was a perfect union, and had been for almost thirty years.

So when Michael switched from NBC to CBS, Kent also made the transition. After all, his allegiance was to Michael, not to a network. Together the two men began working on a new series pilot, which they would shoot during the last two months of 1990. Titled "Us," the show was to star Michael as a recently released convict, trying to pick up the pieces of his life, which included an ex-wife and a son he'd never seen, despite the objections of his father, portrayed by Barney Martin. Michael had written the pilot script in less than ten days. With that accomplished, Kent was busily involved in preproduction for the two-hour movie that, when released, would spell success or failure for the series.

In the meantime, Michael was determined to slow down and spend the intervening months with Cindy and the children. Besides, the family had just moved from their $6 million beach house into their new home, a $7 million, 11,000-square-foot, two-story Mediterranean villa big enough to comfortably embrace the entire Landon clan, set on ten acres of prime real estate in a Malibu canyon. Since it had taken more than two years to build, Michael was determined to enjoy the dream house, with its acreage, its swimming pool, and its privacy.

It was an idyllic couple of months for Cindy, Michael, and the children; a time of barbecues, fishing, swimming, playing with the various members of the family's menagerie, which then included four horses and nine dogs, and making videos of it all. Then there were the times when, as always, the family—and any friends who happened to be visiting—would hop in the car to go rent videos and get carryout from one of the restaurants along the Pacific Coast Highway, or PCH as it's known to locals.

"I always dreamed of some day having a wife and family where there would be peace, love, and tranquility," Michael said. "Cindy, the children, the house . . . I've gotten everything I ever wanted. I'm a very happy man."

Having agreed to slow down, Michael also agreed to do some traveling. He couldn't take an entire year off to travel the world with his family as Cindy had suggested, but he did agree to take several shorter educational trips. Cindy planned a mid-June trip to the Gallapagos Islands, just before he would begin working on the new series. And later, the couple, along with the kids, were planning a journey to Africa, which Michael had always described as "my favorite place, aside from home."

"I couldn't be an actor or director," Michael had once confessed. "I would have liked to have been a guide in Africa, traveling around photographing wild animals in their natural habitat, spending all my time in the bush."

So with the family's foreseeable future planned, and with Kent McCray serving as line producer, Michael and his new costars filmed the two-hour pilot of "Us" during November and December of 1990, wrapping shortly before Christmas.

Michael was pleased with the show, but he was still worried about its acceptance, not only from the viewers but from his new partners at CBS, namely Jeff Sagansky, the network's president.

Unlike Tartikoff, with whom Landon had become friends and who had once publicly stated that his "dream network would be twenty-two hours of Michael Landon programs," Sagansky was a new personality in Michael's life. And Michael did not easily warm up to new people. Thus Michael was cautious in his conversations with Sagansky. Even though the CBS programming executives had enthusiastically embraced the pilot, and had assured Michael the series would be on the network's fall 1991 schedule, it was his nature to remain skeptical.

Michael felt comfortable only with his small coterie of long-term friends, which is why he attended few Hollywood parties and even fewer Hollywood functions. Away from family and friends, he became Eugene Orowitz, that shy, nervous, insecure little fellow who was uncomfortable in his own skin. Those were feelings that Michael never managed to escape. He preferred to stay at home and to keep most outside relationships either at arm's length or on a strictly professional level.

After wrapping up the pilot in December, however, Michael did discuss the show with a newspaper writer. "It's not a show where you're going to be able to guess what's going to happen," he had explained. "It's like life really is."

After the holidays, life returned to its normal pace, with Michael still getting up at an hour most people would consider the middle of the night, and Cindy getting up not much later to get Jennifer and Sean ready for school.

"Cindy is a good mother," Michael would tell anyone who would listen. "She gets up at 5:45 A.M., gets the kids dressed, then gets their breakfast and drives them to school. I can afford to have servants do all that, but she doesn't want anybody else taking care of her children. She piles them in the car and drives them to school, then drives back and picks them up in the afternoon. She drives them everywhere — to the doctor, the dentist, their friends' houses, to Jennifer's Brownie troop meetings.

"Last year she even won an award from the Brownies for being the mother who drove all the kids to the most places," he had proudly added, more like a proud father than a dazzled husband.

In March 1991, Michael decided the family should go skiing. It would only be for a week, but it would also be the only break he'd get until June, thanks to the production schedule of "Us." Everybody, from the kids to Cindy, was thrilled. So the family took off for Park City, Utah, for fun and games on the ski slopes. But despite his carefree demeanor, Michael was worried. So worried that he didn't even confide in Cindy. He had been having severe stomach pains for several weeks and they were getting worse.

Convinced that he probably had developed an ulcer, Michael had gone to the doctor and had an upper GI done just prior to the family's departure for Utah. The tests had shown nothing except for an unusual amount of stomach acid. So the physician had given him some antacid pills. Like Michael, he had decided the cramps were probably stress-related.

In Park City, however, the pain worsened. Finally unable to stand the stabbing pain in his abdomen, Michael flew back to Los Angeles a day early, leaving Cindy and the children in Utah. He checked into Cedars-Sinai medical center the following day, April 3, to have a CAT scan done.

"I knew something was wrong," he would later tell the press, "when the doctor told me he would check the results and call me around ten-thirty that night. Sure enough, he called and he said, 'You had better get Cindy back here.' And I said, 'What have I got?' "

It was then that Michael learned he had a large tumor in his abdomen. Whether it was malignant or benign would not be determined until the following day, when a biopsy had been scheduled.

On Friday, April 5, only two days after his flight from Park City to Los Angeles, the diagnosis was in, and it wasn't good. Cindy and Michael heard the news together: Michael had adenocarcinoma, the medical name for cancer of the pancreas. It was inoperable and had already spread to his liver. Michael was stunned. He had never expected anything like this.

After all, the only other time in his life he'd been really sick had been in 1974, when he got encephalitis and his temperature had risen to almost 107 degrees. The doctors had told Lynn that Michael might not survive; and they had added, if he *did* live chances were the high temperature would have created brain damage. But Michael had fooled everyone. Not only did he live, he had suffered no brain damage, and although the doctors had said he wouldn't be able to work for at least six months, that he'd be too weak, he'd returned to the set only a week after the temperature had broken.

But this? This was different. This was frightening.

"Are you sure?" Michael asked, gripping the arms of his chair. "I mean I was feeling fine until a month ago."

When the doctor nodded his head, Michael swallowed hard, trying to maintain his composure. Cindy grasped his hand and began to cry. Later, alone in the bedroom of their Malibu dream house, they cried together.

The following evening, Michael gathered his entire family together for what they believed to be a routine family dinner. Everyone, according to a close friend, was in a happy mood, glad that Cindy and their dad were back. There was a lot of laughing, a lot of teasing, as was the norm when all of the kids got together. Then Michael, who had been sitting at the head of the table, stood up, a serious look on his face. And he told them the bad news.

There was a moment of silence as everyone in the room processed what he was saying, and then there was pandemonium as they raced to embrace Michael. Michael understood there had to be tears but he didn't want that kind of response beyond that night. He had made up his mind, and he told them he was going to need their support. He was going to fight this cancer, this invasion of his body, with every ounce of strength he had. He was not going to succumb to defeatism. He was going to meet this challenge on the same stubborn basis he'd met all other challenges throughout his life: With strength, candor, humor, and the will to win, to overcome, to triumph. He was, after all, Michael Landon, a man who had played an angel on television, a man who believed in the power of the mind, a man who believed in miracles. He could do no less for himself and his family than to face this obstacle with courage and determination. He could be no less for his fans, the viewing public.

With that, Michael mentally rolled up his shirtsleeves, and faced the greatest challenge of his life the only way he knew how: Head on. The man who had produced miracles on "Highway to Heaven" for five consecutive years had suddenly found himself searching for his own private miracle.

Sixteen

Realizing it would be only a short while before the press unearthed the fact of his illness, Michael decided to hold a press conference in an attempt to prevent the usual wild and speculative stories for which the tabloid press is noted. By holding a press conference and actually announcing his illness, as well as openly, candidly fielding questions about it, Michael believed he could spare his family the morbid flurry of doom and gloom reportage that usually accompanied the travails of celebrities.

On Monday, April 8, only three days after learning of his illness, Michael called a press conference through his publicist and spokesman, John Flynn, who wisely scheduled it so that the news would break that night on television. A half hour before the conference was scheduled to begin, reporters from the Los Angeles area newspapers, as well as from the wire services and magazines, began making their way through the gate and up the drive to the Landon house. The TV crews set up their cameras, and the still photographers worked their way around them, looking for a spot from which to get the best photos. Despite all of the activity, no one knew exactly what it was that Michael Landon was going to announce. They only knew there had been rumors that he was ill and that he had something important to discuss. Still, they were unprepared for what followed when Michael finally appeared before them.

Wearing a neatly pressed bright green shirt and khaki pants, Michael walked out on the patio of his two-story Malibu home, with its red-tiled roofs and colonnades, and sat down, facing the barrage of press, on a cushioned wrought iron patio chair. He was, some of the press noted, a little thinner than they had remembered. But he still looked great, with his long hair framing his bronzed, handsome face.

"My God!" he exclaimed when he first saw the dozen or so reporters and cameramen gathered by his front yard pool. "Boy, you gotta be real sick to get this much attention." It was the beginning of an emotional half-hour press conference, punctuated with humor and tinged with sadness.

Obviously uncomfortable yet trying to appear at ease, Michael attempted to lighten the atmosphere by cracking his usual brand of sarcastic jokes.

"I want my agent to know that this shoots to hell any chance of doing a health food commercial," he quipped shortly after explaining to the astonished press that he had been diagnosed with inoperable cancer of the pancreas and liver.

He followed that joke by admitting his role as an angel on "Highway to Heaven" might have helped him adjust to his current situation because "I played a dead guy anyway." But despite Michael's valiant attempt to lighten the mood, nobody laughed, and after noting that he had "a sense of humor about everything," Michael had to swallow hard to go on. There was more than just a hint of sadness in his eyes, as he began seriously discussing his illness.

"I don't find this particularly funny," he began anew, "but if you are going to try to beat something, you are not going to do it standing in the corner. I think all of us create our own miracles.

"At first you just don't believe it, especially if you are a physical kind of guy," he continued. "So what I did right after I heard there was a possibility, was I began doing push-ups, just to make sure I was just as strong as I was the day before. And I was, so I figured I could beat it."

At that point, he did several push-ups at the urging of the press, but was visibly fatigued afterward. Returning to his chair, Michael brought up the subject of his CBS series, "Us."

"It's kind of a dirty trick to do to your costars when they finally get a break and the series sells," he said, adding, "There is no way for me to continue with that right now until we determine whether or not this chemo is going to help me or not."

"Right now," he continued, "I feel terrific. The only difficulty I have is in digesting food, so I have become a papaya juice lover. You don't gain a hell of a lot of weight drinking papaya juice," he said, explaining that his ideal weight had been 160 pounds, that he had been losing weight and, at that point, was down to 154 pounds.

"Life has been good to me," he concluded. "It's not like I missed an awful lot. I had a pretty good lick here. I am going to fight it. Every moment gets a little more important after something like this. So, live every minute, guys."

With that, Michael stood up and slowly walked back toward the patio door to his house. Reaching the doorway, he turned for a moment, raised a defiant fist, then disappeared from view. The TV crews packed up their equipment in silence and the print reporters left quietly. It had been a poignant, unforgettable meeting and even the most hardened members of the press had to admit that Michael had been brave and touchingly forthright. Only his tightened lips, taut chin, and the deep sadness in his eyes had reflected his underlying stress. Other than that, Michael Landon had looked fantastic, especially for being fifty-four years old. He certainly did not look like a man on the brink of death.

And yet Michael was ill, very ill.

According to the American Cancer Society, only three percent of pancreatic cancer patients and five percent of liver cancer patients survive more than five years after diagnosis. "Cancer of the pancreas," acknowledged Dr. Gerald Murphy, chief medical officer for the American Cancer Society, "is a silent disease that occurs without symptoms until it is in its advanced stages."

The news of Michael's illness hit the network television newscasts later that night, with NBC devoting more than usual coverage to the press conference. After all, Michael had been a mainstay of the network for almost three decades. Even though he had moved to CBS, it was still impossible to separate him from the NBC peacock. Joining in the coverage, CNN carried the story to the rest of the world on their thirty-minute "Headline News" telecasts throughout the rest of the night.

"I heard about his illness on the news," said Hal Burton, "and it just made me sick. I turned on every station and, well, it was like dropping a rock on me. I couldn't believe it then and can barely believe it now. He's been like a brother to me. I mean, if it hadn't been for Michael my career probably never would have gotten off the ground. He gave a lot of people their first breaks."

All of the coverage was essentially the same, with footage of Michael discussing his situation at the press conference backed up with a brief statement concerning his hospitalization, by Ron Wise, spokesman for Cedars-Sinai:

"Michael has an enormous amount of fight in him, and in my experience that has a lot to do with how things go. He doesn't impress me as the kind of guy who will throw in the towel, and his doctors are not quitters. He's a strong guy, and he's got a great attitude about this. He said he's going to beat it, and I have no reason to doubt that."

By the following morning every newspaper in the country was running the story, which was the biggest entertainment news item of the year. By the next day, there was hardly anyone in America who hadn't either heard or read about Michael's physical ailment. Even people who weren't Michael Landon fans were stunned by the news. It was almost impossible to believe that someone as virile, as handsome, as healthy-looking, and as youthful as Michael could be that ill. It was also difficult to imagine someone having the grace, the courage, the forthrightness to stand up in front of the world and candidly describe his potentially fatal illness. But Michael had done just that and it had touched the hearts of millions of viewers, not just those who were fans.

By the end of the week, Michael had begun receiving thousands of cards and letters, as well as Bibles, from people he had never met, all of whom had been moved by his illness and his determination to fight what was most likely a losing battle.

"I got a phone call from a friend who had heard about it on the radio," Merlin Olson later recalled. "My first reaction was disbelief. I thought he must have heard wrong, that it couldn't have been accurate because I had seen Michael not long before that and he had looked so healthy, so vigorous. I was working on the satellite, going back and forth, a couple of minutes later and, suddenly, there was Michael at the press conference.

"At that point, of course, I knew it was true, but it was still very difficult to accept because Michael was always so conscious of keeping in shape."

Michael would later confess, however, that he was aware the cancer could have been caused by his years of heavy smoking and poor dietary habits.

"The news shocked me," he would admit in an exclusive *Life* magazine article published in June, 1991. "Nothing was further from my mind, since I'm only fifty-four and, with rare exceptions, I'd been healthy my whole life. Not that I don't deserve to have a cancer. I'm a good athlete, and I work out hard—before this happened I could bench press three hundred, three hundred and fifty pounds, no sweat—but I've abused my body over the years. I think I have it because for most of my life, though I was never a drunk, I drank too much. I also smoked too many cigarettes and ate a lot of wrong things. And if you do that, even if you think you're too strong to get anything, somehow you're going to pay."

Although Michael had initially agreed to undergo chemotherapy for the cancer, he changed his mind after having had the first treatment only days after his press conference. He had hated it. He hated the thought of being injected with poisonous chemicals. He hated the idea of not being in control of his life. So he decided to change courses, even though his medical doctors were recommending chemo as his only hope, and embraced a holistic program of diet and exercise.

On April 14 he had met with Dr. Charles Simone of Lawrenceville, N.J., an oncologist noted for using a combination of traditional and non-traditional healing methods to attack cancer. Michael was told that Dr. Simone had been involved in Ronald Reagan's colon cancer treatments when Reagan had been in the White House. Dr. Simone's nontraditional plan was mainly dietary, such as eating healthy foods, taking vitamins and getting as much exercise as possible, along with stress management techniques, such as hypnosis.

After a lengthy discussion with Simone, Michael optimistically launched into the program. Once a steak and lobster man who ate little during the day and devoured lumberjack portions of heavy foods at dinner, he adhered to a daily diet-and-exercise routine that consumed a great portion of his day.

The diet called for Michael to consume organic apples and carrots and beet tops, all of which he would toss in the blender to create a twelve-ounce glass of juice, which he would drink at least a dozen times a day. He became consumed with reading about nutrition, how it worked within the body. "The pectin in the apples helps the digestion," he would explain to anyone who inquired. "Most of the vegetables I'm eating are high in enzymes to replace the digestive juices my pancreas has stopped producing. And the carotene in the carrots is supposed to kill cancer cells but," he would add with a laugh, "those damn carrots are turning me orange."

In addition, Michael took coffee enemas and, following Dr. Simone's regimen, ate only organic foods — lentils, beans and raw vegetables — three times a day.

Michael and Cindy were overjoyed when, after a couple of days, the stomach pains subsided and Michael was able to eat lightly but comfortably again. He regained some of the weight he'd lost and he had more energy. He was playing some tennis and still working out, although not as heavily as he had in the past. "Thank God," he confided to his close friends, "Cindy is a health nut and knows about nutrition because she can make the most wonderful soups out of basically nothing."

Despite his optimism and his dedication to the diet, however, less than two weeks after his diagnosis, he could tell he was weaker than he had been. So Michael decided he should save his energy and tapered off from any physical exercise, including his morning push-ups and afternoon tennis games.

"I'm convinced I'm doing the right thing for me," he told friends, adding, "but we'll see. I'm going to stick with the program for a month or so and then see what happens. If the cancer hasn't stopped growing by then, I'll reevaluate."

At that point, most of Michael's thoughts and conversation were about his health, experimental treatments for cancer and the pros and cons of the holistic approach to medicine. Every telephone conversation he had dealt solely with those subjects. It was tiring but Michael nevertheless would patiently explain the illness to friends.

"The CAT scan," he would repeatedly explain, "shows two spots on my liver, one about half an inch, the other an inch, and another spot near my kidneys. The tumor on the pancreas is about the size of a softball, and it's pressing against my stomach, which is what's been causing the cramps and making it impossible for me to eat much. So," he'd add with a sardonic smile, "I'm not going to pretend I have a hangnail. This kind of cancer is almost always fatal, and when you go you usually go fast. The deterioration is swift."

Michael had given himself six weeks to see if the program would work. If the cancer hadn't been halted by then, he and Cindy had agreed that he would reevaluate the situation and seriously consider entering into a program of chemotherapy. In the meantime, the diet was building up his immune system and he had already begun taking hormones to increase his dwindling red cell count.

"The purpose of all this," he explained to his children, "is to build up my resistance so that the doctors can try some new experimental procedures on me. They don't know if they'll work, but, hey, what have I got to lose?"

Upon learning of his illness, Michael's first response after accepting the seriousness of his situation was to curtail all activities, except those involving his health and his family. He wanted to spend whatever remaining days he had with Cindy and the children, especially his two youngest children, Jennifer and Sean. So, during the early days of the battle, he would accompany Cindy when she drove the kids to and from school. He went to several Little League games with Sean, and he went to see Jennifer dance in a school recital.

"I have absolutely no fear of dying," Michael told his friends. "I've had a good life, better than most people, in fact. What bothers me," he had confided, "is not getting to see Jennifer and Sean grow up and leaving Cindy with two young kids. I think all of this is harder on my family than it is on me."

Always open with his children, Michael was even more open, more demonstrative in the days following that Saturday evening when he had calmly explained the situation to his family. He spent hours with Jennifer and Sean, and he explained to them, trying to ease the fear he could sometimes see on their little faces, how hard he was fighting *not* to leave them.

"I told them that what I had they couldn't catch. I told them that even if I were to die, they would be fine. They would miss me terribly, and I would miss them terribly, but that nothing would change. They would still live in the same house and their friends would still be the same; and that their mother would be there, and that she was young and strong and so they would be safe."

It was, Michael later told a close family friend, more difficult for him to deal with the pain and puzzlement of his children than it was for him to endure his own ordeal. But he nevertheless remained strong and confident, explaining each step he was taking, and why, as he faced the future. He was carefully nurturing the children while, at the same time, preparing them for what he knew awaited him.

Two weeks after having begun Dr. Simone's program of diet and exercise, Michael and Cindy summarily disavowed any affiliation with him after learning that there was some question concerning the extent of Dr. Simone's involvement in the treatment of Ronald Reagan's colon cancer. They were also unhappy that Dr. Simone had suddenly acquired star status and had begun appearing on television and radio talk shows, discussing his treatment for cancer patients such as Michael.

On April 24 Michael had gone in for a second CAT scan to see if any progress had been made in his fight against the cancer. Since he'd been feeling fairly well, he was optimistic throughout the procedure . . . and totally unprepared for the results: The cancer had spread, and the tumor had almost doubled in size.

It was, a close family friend recalled, the only time during his three-month illness that Michael emotionally crashed. "It's only a matter of weeks now," he confided to his family and friends.

Seventeen

When Michael had called his press conference on April 8 to announce his illness, he had hoped that his open and frank discussion of the cancer would prelude the usual tabloid headlines, all of which titillated the public but created ongoing pain for the families of those about whom they were writing. It quickly became apparent, however, that this was not going to be the case. Michael Landon, his family, and friends, had overnight become hot news, grist for the weekly tabloid doses of doom and gloom.

Michael had known the chance he was taking by coming out in the open with the news of his illness. But his father had been a publicist and Michael had long understood the publicity game. He knew that to attempt to keep the news under wraps would only serve to create fiction. He realized that the only way he could control what was written about him and his family was to give the press the entire story as it unraveled. Nevertheless, he was unprepared for a banner headline in the *National Enquirer* which read in glaring huge capital letters: MICHAEL LANDON: IT'S OVER!

Furious about the headline, and even angrier over the story which purported to relate conversations between him and Cindy and their children, Michael telephoned his friend, Johnny Carson, on Monday, May 6, and asked if he would be interested in having him as a guest on the "Tonight Show." The normally casual Carson was stunned by the call, and pleased. Of course he would like to have Michael on the show. Everyone wanted Michael Landon for an interview—the newspapers, magazines, television networks. The whole world was waiting, and would be watching, to see what was coming next in Michael's proclaimed battle against a cancer known to be especially ravaging.

After checking with his "Tonight Show" talent coordinators to see who was scheduled to be on the show that week, meaning who could be gracefully bumped from one night to another, Johnny called Michael back. How would he like to be on the show Thursday? Michael said that would be fine, the sooner the better. The following day, Harry Flynn, Michael's spokesman, was quoted in a story that ran in *The Hollywood Reporter*, announcing Michael's "Tonight Show" appearance two days hence, on Thursday, May 9.

"He wanted to go somewhere where he could

show people he isn't all that sick," Flynn explained. "He wants people to know he's hanging in there despite the deathbed stories appearing in the tabs. He wanted to go on a show and lighten up," Flynn said, adding, "It will not be maudlin. It will be fun."

And so on Thursday afternoon, almost a month to the date of his press conference, Michael drove through the gates of the NBC studios in Burbank, arriving without incident at the artist's entrance, for the 4:30 P.M. taping of the show. Stepping out of the car, Michael was immediately surrounded by network security guards plus a special contingent of Pinkerton security people, who lined the corridor leading from the entrance to Studio One, where the "Tonight Show" is always taped.

Aware there was a rumor floating through Hollywood that one of the tabloids had offered $50,000 to any photographer able to get a shot of Landon at the taping, NBC had doubled its usual amount of security to make sure no paparazzi managed to get through security and onto the lot. As a result, Michael's entrance and exit were uneventful, except for a brief well-wishes of the "Tonight Show" audience, most of them out-of-towners, who were shocked to see Michael walking past them on his way into the studio. Having procured their tickets to the show months ago, they had no idea who would be appearing on the program that night.

So the audience waited patiently as Ed McMahon warmed them up, and the orchestra began tuning their instruments, because they knew they had somehow managed to stumble into a moment of television history, something they would never forget, something to tell their neighbors back home, something to tell their grandchildren.

At the appointed hour, the band struck up the show's opening theme, Ed's familiar voice did his introduction, and Carson appeared from behind the curtains to launch into his monologue. Then, less than fifteen minutes into the show, Johnny began his introduction of his good friend, Michael Landon.

"As you've probably heard," Carson began, "Michael Landon recently announced that he had inoperable cancer of the pancreas and liver and that would stun anybody. But like Michael Landon, he met the problem head-on. He invited the press to his house and told them the situation. He did that mainly to avoid the rumors, the speculation, the misinformation; and to try to avoid sensationalism by the tabloids. And for the past month he has continued to face this battle with humor, honesty, and a personal sense of dignity that characterizes the man. Would you welcome, Michael Landon . . ."

Wearing a bright turquoise-colored shirt and light beige pants, Michael appeared from behind the curtains. He was greeted by a lengthy round of applause and wild cheering from the studio audience. A piece of television history was in the making.

"It's good to see you," Carson began as soon as

Michael had taken his seat. Normally cool, calm, and collected, especially after his more than thirty years as the "Tonight Show" host, Carson was obviously nervous and ill at ease as the two men began chatting. Michael, on the other hand, seemed perfectly at ease.

"It's good to see you," he said, leaning toward Carson.

"I was really rather touched when you called and said you wanted to be on this show because I know every show in the country has been calling you to come on. And I'm very flattered that you're here."

"Well," Michael replied, "you're my buddy, man."

Then, after a couple of minutes of small talk, Michael turned the conversation to the reason he had decided to do the show.

"The thing I want to clear up right away is the tenth child business," he said, adding. "There's a big headline in one of those incredible tabloid magazines about the fact that I want to have a tenth child so my wife will have something to remember me by. Here I've got nine kids, nine dogs, three grandkids — and one in the oven — three parrots . . . and my wife, Cindy, needs something to remember me by?"

Michael laughed, as did the audience and the great joke master himself, Carson. Through his unflinching sense of humor, Michael had managed to make everyone feel at ease. And as Harry Flynn had stated only two days before, the program was essentially a light-hearted romp, with

Michael discussing his illness and the response he'd received from the public.

"I really want to thank everybody," Michael said at one point. "I've received a lot of great suggestions and I'm using a little bit of everything. Although," he added with a sly grin, "there were some suggestions I didn't try. One guy wrote me and told me that the reason I got the Big C was that I did not get enough sex. See, he thinks it was only the nine times when I had the kids. So he said as soon as I . . . well, he gave me the regimen, which would kill the average twenty-five-year-old. So, I gotta really get the red count up to accomplish what I need to accomplish to get well, because this guy wants to open a clinic for guys who . . . well, he says if you don't have sex more than twice a week you're gonna get it."

"Hmm," Carton responded, "a strange man. How many suggestions like this have you received?"

"Oh, there's thousands. I've gotten tapes, books, you name it," Michael replied. "I even got a tip about swimming with a dolphin. You only have to do it once. Something about sonar from the dolphin and — bing, bing — it goes away. What can I tell you? Here I'm going to all these hospitals and I only gotta go to Marineland!"

In between commercial breaks, the two men discussed everything from Landon's coffee enemas ("I invited John over for a coffee enema, but he wanted cream and sugar, and I'm not pouring!" Landon chuckled to the delight of the audience.)

198

to the fact that he had been dying his hair for years. ("I had my roots done yesterday," Michael laughed, after Carson commented on how nice his hair looked.)

They discussed the Norman Cousins book, *Anatomy of An Illness*, and the effect humor can have on a major illness. And Carson told about the time Michael had pulled a prank on him by convincing him he had run over the owner's cat in the parking lot of the Beaurivage restaurant, a trendy Malibu restaurant, then inviting him back to the restaurant a month later.

"I told him, 'I don't know if I really want to go there, Mike, maybe they'll be mad at me,' " Carson told the audience, adding, "but he said, 'Oh, c'mon, let's go.' "

So the two met for dinner and, as Carson recalled, the waiter brought the menu, a fancy menu done in old English script. "So I'm reading the menu," Carson begins, "and I see 'Turine of Tabby' listed under Soups. Then I keep reading and under appetizers I see 'Pussy Mousse à la Mercedes.' I go to the next page, where the entrees are listed, and I see 'Pressed Pussy Provencal' and under it, in tiny letters, it says: 'served outside in the dark.' "

The show moved swiftly as the two men continued bantering back and forth. Talking about his latest project, Michael had brought a scene from the CBS pilot, "Us," which the network had planned on adding to their September 1991 schedule. "I called Jeff Sagansky at CBS and told him, 'If I don't get better, this is the worst mistake you'll have made since buying baseball,' " Michael laughed.

Although the pilot had been shot only five months before, there was a noticeable difference in Michael's looks. He looked older, more gaunt on the "Tonight Show" and there was a set to his jaw that hadn't been there when he had appeared in the series pilot.

By the end of the "Tonight Show," Michael looked fatigued. He had been upbeat throughout the show, however, except for a brief moment when, at the end of Carson's interview with fellow guest, boxer George Foreman, he had seized the opportunity to inject a somber note into the otherwise light-hearted show. Taking the nation's tabloids to task for printing lurid headlines about his cancer and stories he said his youngest children had read and been frightened by, Michael turned to the audience. His face was grim and he was obviously angry.

"It's unbelievable that people can be that way," he said, referring specifically to a tabloid story which had stated he had only four weeks left to live. "That's the cancer, you know. That's the cancer in our society."

The show ended only minutes later, with Michael giving a smile and a farewell wave to the audience who, in turn, gave him a standing ovation.

No one, outside of Michael, Cindy, and his doctors, could possibly have suspected it would be

Michael's last official public appearance. And it did make television history.

According to the Nielsen ratings, it was the most-watched "Tonight Show" of the last ten years, and the second highest rated segment of the show aired since Carson took over its reins in 1962. In terms of viewership, it had been topped only by the 1968 televised wedding of Tiny Tim and Miss Vicki.

Eighteen

After appearing on the "Tonight Show," Michael became reclusive, spending all of his time at home with Cindy and the children. "I only have X amount of energy," he told friends, "and I want to spend it with my family."

Despite an increasing flow of phone calls from friends and acquaintances, all wanting to express their concern, each hoping to convey their wish for his speedy recovery, no one but a few close friends like Kent McKay, Harry Flynn, and other family members, ever saw or spoke to Michael again.

Brandon Tartikoff was one of the few concerned well-wishers who did manage to talk to Michael shortly after his illness became public. Tartikoff had also been backstage at the "Tonight

202

Show" to personally wish Michael a speedy recovery.

"I first heard about Michael's illness from a friend who called me on my car phone, while I was driving to the hospital to visit my daughter, who's going through rehab from the car accident we had. My friend wanted to know if I'd seen the morning news, and I hadn't. So I immediately turned on the car radio and, of course, there it was," Tartikoff would later recall.

"I was devastated," he continued. "It's real hard to imagine life, TV, my world, without Michael Landon because he's always been such a permanent fixture. He's always been a fountain of eternal youth. He's always been everybody's father image. He's always been brimming with life and health.

"Since I had been through the cancer experience personally, with Hodgkin's disease, my immediate response to Michael's illness was to ask myself, 'What can I do to help him tip the odds?' Whatever I could do for Michael became my immediate agenda.

"I immediately wrote him a letter and then talked to him on the phone," Tartikoff continued, adding, "I was surprised and delighted to learn that he was already ahead of me in fighting that kind of illness. Michael was incredibly positive and was attacking it the same way I did. My first reaction upon learning I had Hodgkin's was that I had to be strong so that I could get through the battle ahead of me.

"My illness was certainly a less ferocious battle

than Michael's," Tartikoff concluded, "but you still have to have the best mind-set to win it. And Michael had that mind-set. He had the spirit of someone who could triumph. He'd always been a very positive, upbeat person and that was going to work very much in his favor in fighting this thing."

On Monday, May 13, Michael underwent his first experimental treatment, where a cancer-killing chemical was put into fat bubbles and then injected directly into his tumor. The procedure was carried out by Dr. Cary Presant, chairman of the Los Angeles Oncologic Institute headquartered at the St. Vincent Medical Center near downtown Los Angeles. Dr. Presant, who reported to the press that Michael had "mild discomfort and fatigue" following the injection, but that "his spirits remain high," then took the naysayers among the press to task.

"It angers me," he said, "to have people establishing a prognosis for Michael, people who have never seen him and who are unfamiliar with his treatment. It also angers Michael. He's expressed that to me."

A week later, Michael collapsed in crippling pain on the floor of the upstairs master bedroom bathroom. Hearing him scream out, Cindy raced to his side and somehow managed to get him into the car. She then sped from their rural home in Malibu to Cedars-Sinai hospital, a thirty-mile drive through rush hour traffic, in less than forty minutes. She was visibly shaken as the emergency room workers gently lifted Michael out of the car, put him in a wheelchair, and then admitted him to a private room.

The pain was obviously severe, said an observer, because Michael seemed to be unable to get his breath. A short while later, the doctors found that he had suffered massive internal bleeding and had blood clots throughout his body, not only near his heart, but in his legs and abdomen, creating pain that was almost unbearable. He was immediately given morphine.

Ironically, as Michael slept away the night at the hospital, with Cindy asleep on a cot in his room, a television special he had filmed several months before, *America's Missing Children*, was telecast that night on the CBS network. The Michael Landon who served as the host of that show bore only a minimal resemblance to the Michael Landon who, wearing a black shirt and black pants, was released from Cedars-Sinai the following Saturday, May 25.

Although the attending physicians claimed the severe clotting was unrelated to the experimental cancer treatment he had undergone only a week before, Michael decided he would forego any further chemotherapy, experimental or otherwise. He looked tired, thin, and haggard when he walked by the clamoring press photographers. He was limping and Cindy had to help him into the car, which she then drove away. It was obvious to everyone there that the disease was taking its toll. It was the beginning of a gradual downward spiral in which Michael would grow increasingly weaker and begin sleeping more.

According to a family friend, it was at that point that Michael told his doctors, "Let's not prolong this hospital thing. I want to die at home." The physicians agreed and an intensive care unit was quickly set up at the Malibu house. A hospital bed, along with oxygen tanks, intravenous devices, morphine, anti-nausea drugs, and blood for transfusions, was delivered the following day. Back home, surrounded by the family he loved, Michael was as happy as he could be under the circumstances.

"Actually not much really changed from the time Michael was diagnosed," confided a close friend. "There were big swings in him, physically, from one day to the next. But, emotionally, he was always up, except for the day he learned from the CAT scan that the tumor had doubled in size. He was crushed and very, very down. But the next day, he was back at it. He was determined not to give in to depression. He wanted to stay mentally up for Cindy and the kids and for himself. And he did.

"He really believed in what he'd said on the 'Tonight Show' about your mental state being fifty percent of the medicine. Of course," the friend added, "the pain medicine took its toll and he slept a lot. It was a real emotional roller coaster for everyone because one day he'd sleep most of the time, then the next day he'd feel fine and be up for dinner. At that point, everybody was overjoyed and excited because he seemed to be back, to be holding his own."

While Michael valiantly tried to bolster his immune system through vitamins, enzymes, acupuncture, visualization, and the experimental treatment with liposomes, his fans seemed to be either watching and waiting, or sending cards and letters. At one point, Michael was receiving more than five thousand a day from well-wishers all over the world. Even *TV Guide* began receiving Michael Landon letters, sent them by readers who knew of no other way to reach their hero.

"My heart goes out to Michael Landon," wrote one reader. "He so often has portrayed human beings acting nobly in the face of adversity; one expects he will face this great challenge nobly."

"He will be an encouragement to me," wrote another reader, who was stricken with multiple sclerosis.

Those fans who *did* know how to locate Michael began dropping letters and cards off at the gate of his Malibu ranch. Some people even went so far as to scrawl "get well" messages on the walls and front gate guarding the family's privacy. Others simply drove slowly by, stopping momentarily for a moment of prayer, while some of them pinned colored ribbons to a large flowering magenta bougainvillea bush just across the road. Nearby, a self-professed mystic had pitched a tent, and was spending his days sitting cross-legged, facing the house, focusing all of his attention on silent prayers twenty-four hours a day for a man he did not know and had never seen except on television.

Amazingly, unlike other similar situations, such as when Rock Hudson and Liberace were rumored to be at death's door, there was never a carnival-like atmosphere outside the Landons' home. Like Michael, the people who were his fans and admirers handled the situation with dignity and grace. They were a living reflection of thirty years of Michael Landon's messages of faith, hope, and charity he had sent so clearly to the world through his television series.

According to several friends, Michael was not only courageous in the face of death, he also was extraordinarily selfless, hoping for a miracle that would cure his illness so that other people suffering from supposedly incurable ailments could take heart.

"I have absolutely no fear of dying," Michael had told them on more than one occasion. "But," he had added, "if I could beat this thing, think what an inspiration that would be to all the other people with supposedly terminal illnesses. It would give hope to millions of people."

During this time, Michael and Cindy had serious talks about how she should handle her life, and that of their two young children, after he was gone. He wanted her to remarry when she was ready and he wanted her to make sure the family stayed together. "I don't want them to split up, or forget each other, or stop seeing each other," he told her. He also asked Kent McCray and John Warren, two of his closest friends and business advisors, to watch over Cindy. "I want her to remarry when she's ready," he told them. "She can't mourn forever."

At the beginning of his battle against cancer,

Michael had read several books on how humor can have a positive effect on ill health. So he had rented comedy videos and cartoons and, together with his family, had watched them hour upon hour, laughing at the comedic high-jinks of everyone from Laurel and Hardy to Steve Martin. Later, on the days he felt up to it, Michael devoted a great deal of his time to producing his own videos in which he not only starred, but directed and edited both sound and picture, as well. They were the last films he would ever create, ever control, but they were far from simply entertaining. They were videos of Michael reading his own will and making absolutely certain that his final wishes would be carried out as per his specific instructions.

"The video tapes were his idea," explained a friend. "Michael wanted to make sure that everything was taken care of the way he wanted. It was also his way of saying goodbye to his family. It was sort of a living legacy for the children, especially Jennifer and Sean. Michael felt awful about not living long enough to see them grown up and married, with their own children. I think that, along with leaving Cindy with two young children to raise, was more upsetting to him than his own imminent death."

Despite growing weaker with each passing day, Michael managed to finish the tapes only days before he became so fatigued that he began sleeping most of the time and was rarely able to join the family for dinner. Yet nobody expected the end to come so rapidly because he was still aware, still conscious of what was going on around him.

"He was telling jokes, he was very lucid, very bright, there was nothing down about it," said Kent McCray, Michael's longtime business associate and close friend. So when Harry Flynn was wondering whether or not to take a week's vacation the first week of July, Michael told him, "Don't be silly. Have a good time. I'll be fine."

With that, Flynn and his wife hopped on a plane the last weekend in June and flew to Martha's Vineyard, where they have a summer home. There days later, Michael's condition deteriorated and he slipped into a coma, slowly sinking deeper and deeper away from the world of which he'd been so much a part.

On Friday, June 28, at Michael's request, Cindy gathered her entire family, as well as their inner circle of friends, at the ranch. From that time on, the group kept a constant vigil at Michael's bedside as the weekend passed.

Then late in the morning of Monday, July 1, Michael suddenly awoke and was magically alert. According to Kent McCray, Michael calmly looked at everyone in the room, then told them: "I love you all very much, but would you all go downstairs and give me some time with Cindy?"

Less than two hours later, Cindy came out of the bedroom and slowly made her way downstairs. Michael was gone. It was one-twenty in the afternoon, less than three months after he had been diagnosed with the cancer.

"It was difficult to believe he was gone," a close friend admitted, "because until the last three days nothing much had changed. It had been an up-and-down thing from the beginning."

One by one Michael's family and friends ascended the stairs leading to the second floor and tearfully entered the bedroom, where he lay silent and still, to offer their farewells. A half hour later, a dark coroner's van slowly made its way past the crowd of TV camera crews again gathered outside the Landons' gate. It was a signal to those watching the passing van that the rumor that Michael Landon was on the brink of dying had been true.

Within minutes, KNBC-TV, the local NBC affiliate, interrupted its regular programming to announce Michael's death, with the other Los Angeles television and radio stations quickly following in line.

Approximately four hours after its arrival, the coroner's van pulled slowly through the gates again. Then one by one the other cars departed, carrying the grief-stricken family members and friends to their homes after a weekend vigil they would neither discuss nor forget.

Stopping his car in the middle of the road, just outside the gates, Michael, Jr., got out and, despite the lurid press coverage by the nation's grocery-store tabloids, thanked the remaining press members for having displayed sensitivity toward the Landon family during the three-month ordeal.

By the time the 11 P.M. newscasters had aired their segments on Michael, he had already been cremated. His memory, however, was very much alive; later that evening on Hollywood Boulevard, where the entire Landon clan had once gathered to watch Michael receive his star on the famous Walk of Fame, people gathered at the same spot to pay their last respects. The Hollywood Chamber of Commerce had placed a wreath in his honor atop the star bearing his name. Other smaller bouquets of flowers had been spread around the area by an array of mourners, young and old.

Harry Flynn, who had been on a plane rushing back to Los Angeles to be at Michael's bedside before the end, spent most of Tuesday dealing with the press, telling them how astounded he had been by how quickly his friend had succumbed.

"He sounded fine when I left," he said, "but then he went downhill in only a matter of three days. The speed of his death was overwhelming. It took your breath away. It was like going off a diving board. He knew it was coming, and he was brave to the last."

As word of Michael's death spread, people who knew him well recalled a man who was a complex individualist of great diversity, a man who was stubborn and sensitive, kind but rough, innovative yet traditional. He was a fighter and a savior and most of all, he was a father figure to generations of Americans.

"In my mind," Brandon Tartikoff said, "there's not a whole lot of difference between the Jonathan Smith character Michael played in 'Highway to Heaven' and the relationship Michael has had with many people, whether on 'Little House,' in movies, or in person. He has come into ordinary people's lives and has had a very special effect on them. And that's because Michael was a very special guy.

"Like many television viewers I grew up with him," Tartikoff continued. "I remember as a kid watching him as 'Little Joe' on 'Bonanza' on the old family Dumont television set. He was at the top of my list then and he remains at the top of my list of special people I have known."

Other Landon intimates recalled the funny side of Michael Landon. "He had a totally warped sense of humor," recalled Alison Arngrim, the young actress who had played Nellie Oleson on 'Little House,' "and he loved elaborate practical jokes, like the time Moses Gunn, the black actor, was on the show."

Landon had surprised Gunn in the middle of a scene, while the cameras were rolling, by appearing out of nowhere, wearing a white KKK hood and carrying a rope.

"Even though he gave the impression of being wholesome and good," Arngrim said, "I think people realized there was a maniacal character underneath. If they didn't see the lunacy showing through," she concluded, "they were in for a big surprise."

Bill Kiley, who had watched Landon grow from being an irrepressible, irresponsible young actor into a mature creative force within the Hollywood community, also found Michael to be a first-class practical joker.

"I'll never, ever forget the time I asked him to hold a little press conference on the last day of 'Bonanza,' " Kiley recalled with a laugh. "He agreed but, without telling me, he rigged himself up in a stuntman's harness, which was designed to yank the bad guys off the set. Well, Michael made a brief statement and then there was a loud shotgun blast and the next thing I knew, he had disappeared. I mean he was gone, totally out of sight. If that wasn't an unforgettable ending to a western series, I don't know what was."

No one, apparently, was safe from the wild and wicked Landon sense of humor, not even Brandon Tartikoff, who was then president and chairman of the NBC Entertainment Group.

As Tartikoff recalled he, along with Michael, Bill Cosby, Johnny Carson, and several other major NBC stars, was returning to Los Angeles from Washington, D.C., where there had been a network affiliates gala, several years ago.

"When I arrived at the airport for the flight," Tartikoff said, "the NBC talent relations man came up to me and said we had a problem and that Michael's flight mistakenly had been canceled and that there wasn't a seat left for him in first class on the flight. I told him, 'Look, I'm exhausted, all I'm going to do is conk out once I'm on the plane. Don't tell Michael any of this, just give him my seat and get me a seat anywhere on the plane.'

"The minute I got into my seat at the back of the plane, I took out my contact lenses and fell asleep. When I awoke hours later, the dinner service was finished. So I called the stewardess and asked if she could get me something to eat. She said she'd be back in a minute.

"Pretty soon I saw, through my blurred vision, a stewardess approaching with a tray of food, and I heard everyone around me start laughing. Well, without my contact lenses in, it looked like a woman in a dress, with long dark hair and clip-on earrings. But it wasn't; it was Michael, who then proceeded to serve me dinner to the amusement of everyone around, myself included."

Five days after Michael's death, on the morning of Friday, July 5, a white stretch limousine, followed by a black limousine, pulled slowly out of the Landon drive. With Cindy and Michael's two youngest children, Jennifer, seven, and Sean, four, in the first car, and his seven other children following close behind, the family headed toward Hillcrest Memorial gardens in West Los Angeles for a memorial service for Michael. Resting prominently on Cindy's lap was a wooden box containing Michael's ashes.

Arriving at the chapel behind the gates of Hillcrest an hour later, Cindy and Michael's family were joined by five hundred other mourners, including former President Ronald Reagan, with whom Michael had once chopped wood, and his wife, Nancy; Merlin Olson, Ernest Borgnine, Brian Keith and many of Michael's costars, such as Melissa Gilbert and Melissa Anderson. Although Michael's first wife, Dodie, accompanied their two sons to the service, his second wife, Lynn, was noticeably absent.

Jay Eller, Michael's close friend and attorney, conducted the service during which many of Michael's friends eulogized him as a loving, kind person, and also recalled his tremendous sense of humor.

According to Leslie Landon, Michael's oldest daughter from his marriage to Lynn, her father had nine dogs and adored every one of them, except for a pooch named Lucy. They didn't get along, Leslie recalled, adding that Michael had told her the one thing that bothered him about dying was that Lucy was going to outlive him. Leslie also confided that, only days before his death, she had told Michael that she knew he would go straight to heaven. "Well," he had laughed, "I don't know if I want to be taken up there right away. I think I'd like some peace and quiet before going up there with everyone."

Then, as a tribute to her father, Leslie read a small poem he'd written years before for an episode of "Little House" about fond remembrance.

In speaking of Michael, Merlin Olson summed him up by saying. "What you say was what you got. Michael was a genuinely loving human being."

Following the memorial service, family and friends moved to another spot, not more than fifty yards from where Michael's beloved TV father, Lorne Greene, had been buried only four years before. With a rabbi conducting the service, Michael's ashes were entombed.

He left an estate estimated worth $100 million and, according to his videotaped will, Cindy was to receive approximately forty percent of his worth, with another forty-percent to be divided among his nine children. The rest was to go to charity, including cancer research.

"Michael Landon," Ronald Reagan had eulogized, "was a man whose tragic battle with cancer touched the hearts of every American, as did his indomitable spirit."

And it had.

Through sheer courage and determination, Michael Landon had imprinted his vision of the American Dream on television viewers throughout the world. Rising from nowhere he had become a living symbol of all that is good, positive and industrious about this country. He was an American visionary, creating a world in which truth, decency and a sense of fairplay prevailed, a land where all things were possible, no matter what the odds. He was, and will remain, an inspiration to anyone seeking to better themselves or to improve upon the world they live in.

CONTEMPORARY FICTION
BY KATHERINE STONE

BEL AIR   (2979, $4.95)
Bel Air—where even the rich and famous are awed by the
wealth that surrounds them. Allison, Winter, Emily: three
beautiful women who couldn't be more different. Three
women searching for the courage to trust, to love. Three women fighting for their dreams in the glamorous and treacherous *Bel Air*.

ROOMMATES   (3355, $4.95)
No one could have prepared Carrie for the monumental
changes she would face when she met her new circle of
friends at Stanford University. Once their lives intertwined
and became woven into the tapestry of the times, they
would never be the same.

TWINS   (2646, $4.50)
Brook and Melanie Chandler were so different, it was hard
to believe they were sisters. One was a dark, serious, ambi-
tious New York attorney; the other, a golden, glamorous,
sophisticated supermodel. But they were more than sisters—they were twins and more alike than even they
knew . . .

THE CARLTON CLUB   (2296, $4.50)
It was the place to see and be seen, the only place to be.
And for those who frequented the playground of the very
rich, it was a way of life. Mark, Kathleen, Leslie and
Janet—they worked together, played together, and loved
together, all behind exclusive gates of the *Carlton Club*.

*Available wherever paperbacks are sold, or order direct from the
Publisher. Send cover price plus 50¢ per copy for mailing and
handling to Zebra Books, Dept. 3651, 475 Park Avenue South,
New York, N.Y. 10016. Residents of New York, New Jersey and
Pennsylvania must include sales tax. DO NOT SEND CASH.*